Henry E. Manning

The True Story Of The Vatican Council

Henry E. Manning

The True Story Of The Vatican Council

ISBN/EAN: 9783337247980

Printed in Europe, USA, Canada, Australia, Japan

Cover: Foto ©Lupo / pixelio.de

More available books at **www.hansebooks.com**

THE TRUE STORY

OF THE

VATICAN COUNCIL.

THE TRUE STORY

OF THE

VATICAN COUNCIL.

BY

HENRY EDWARD,
CARDINAL ARCHBISHOP OF WESTMINSTER.

HENRY S. KING & CO., LONDON.
1877.

PREFACE.

THIS brief Story of the Vatican Council was written at the request of two lay friends, who thought that a true and sufficient estimate of the Council was seldom to be found in what is called public opinion. I call it a Story, because to write a History of the Vatican Council would be the work of a man's life. Slight as I know it to be, I know it also to be true. The facts narrated rest partly upon the authority of the Archbishop of Florence, and none can be more amply provided with documents; and partly upon that of the Secretary of the Council, the Bishop of St. Polten. To this I may also add that, for many details, I have before me the Diary of a very learned and distinguished Bishop present in the Council; and also my own knowledge of facts of which I was personally a witness.

ARCHBISHOP'S HOUSE,
WESTMINSTER, *September 8th*, 1877.

CONTENTS.

CHAPTER I.

First thought of holding an Œcumenical Council proposed by Pius IX.—Commission given to certain Cardinals.—Their answers. — Commission of Direction. — Cardinals and Theologians, Roman and Foreign.—Interrogatories to the Bishops.— Their Answers.—True motive of the Vatican Council an adequate remedy to the disorders, intellectual and moral, of the Christian world. — Disintegration of Europe, and impending dangers, . . pp. 1-40

CHAPTER II.

Eighteenth Centenary of St. Peter's Martyrdom.—The assemblage of 500 Bishops in Rome a powerful cause of the Definition.—First announcement of the Future Council.—Address of the Bishops.—Council of Florence.—Historical outline of the Infallibility.—Bull of Indiction, June 29, 1868.—Conspiracy against the Council. —Diplomatic agitation.—Prince Hohenlohe.—Commission of Direction.—Partition of work. —Letters to the Bishops of the Oriental Churches, and to the new Catholic bodies of the West.—Constitution to regulate the Council.—Subjects to be treated.—Infallibility set aside, ... pp. 41-84

CHAPTER III.

Opening of the Council, Dec. 8, 1869.—Bishop Fessler.—Cardinal de Reisach.—Commission of Postulates.—Commissions of Faith, Discipline, and Religious Orders.—First Public Session.—Profession of Faith.—Method of Discussion, and voting of amendments and reports in the General Congregations.—First Constitution on Catholic Faith passed unanimously in the Second Public Session, and confirmed by

Pius IX.—*Schema* on the Church of Christ.—Petitions for and against the introduction of the Infallibility.—Reasons for and against.—Conclusion of the Majority.—Petition granted.—Chapter on Infallibility, added to the Scheme on March 7, 1870.—Synopsis of the First Constitution on Catholic Faith.—Intellectual aberrations in Philosophy.—Society and Science subject to Faith, . pp. 85-135

CHAPTER IV.

Discussion of the *Schema* on the Church.—On the Infallibility. —Sixty-four Speakers.—A hundred inscribed to speak on General Discussions.—Five Special Discussions still to come. —Closing of General Discussion.—Amendments, and final vote in General Congregation on July 13th.—Protest of Cardinal Presidents.—Fourth Public Session, July 18th.— First Constitution on the Church of Christ passed and confirmed by the Pope.—Franco-German war broke out on the next day.—Opposition in the Council.—Exultation and disappointment of the world.—Defeat of rationalistic intrigues by Bishops of Rottenburg and Mayence.—Freedom of the Council.—Archbishops of Paris and of Cologne.—Tumults and tragedies in the Council.—Cardinal Vitelleschi, Pomponio Leto.—Bishop Strossmayer.—Unity of the Episcopate throughout the World, . . pp. 136-166

CHAPTER V.

The Text of the Definition of the Infallibility of the Roman Pontiff.—What it does not mean.—What it does mean.— Apotheosis. — Deification. — Divine Attributes. — Divine Nature, and other absurdities.—Decree of the Council of Florence.—Evidence of Original MS.—Reasons for the remodelling of the Constitution, and for its speedy discussion. —Consequences imputed to the Council.—Failure of Old Catholic Schism.—True effects of the Council, like those of Trent, to be seen hereafter.—Unity and solidity of the Church to be seen now, . . . pp. 167-206

The True Story of the Vatican Council.

CHAPTER I.

THE ORIGIN AND MOTIVE OF THE VATICAN COUNCIL.

FEW centuries since the Christian era have seen events of greater magnitude or more far-reaching in consequence, than the age in which we live. It has seen the extinction in 1806 of the Holy Roman Empire, the heir and representative of the Cæsars; The rise and fall of two Empires in France; the setting up of two French republics; the overthrow of more dynasties, and the abdication of more kings, than any former age. It is, characteristically, the century of revolution. It has seen great wars which shook the whole of Europe from Madrid to Moscow; and lately two great empires overthrown in a few weeks or in fewer months. It sees now a German Emperor and a king of Italy. Once it has seen the head of the Christian Church carried away prisoner into France, once driven by bloodshed out of Rome, and now we see him stripped of all the world can clutch; twice it has seen Rome seized and held. These are not common events. Finally, after a lapse of three hundred years, it has seen an Œcumenical Council, and it has occupied itself profusely and perpetually about its acts, its liberty, and its decrees. Few events of the nineteenth century stand out in bolder relief, and many will be forgotten when the Vatican Council will be remembered. It will mark this age as the Council of Nicæa and the Council of Trent now mark in history the fourth and the sixteenth centuries. Therefore it will not perhaps be without use, nor, it may be, without interest, if we review its history.

The title prefixed to these pages implies that many stories of the Vatican Council have been published which are not true. It is not my intention to enumerate them. As far as I am able I shall avoid reference to them. My purpose is to narrate the history of the Council, simply and without controversy, from authentic sources. In the present chapter I shall narrate only the origin of the intention to convoke the Council. Hereafter I hope to show what were the antecedents of the Council and their effect upon it; then I will endeavour to explain its acts, and lastly to trace out the effects which have followed from it.

I. In the year 1873 Pius the Ninth gave commission to Eugenio Cecconi, then canon of the Metropolitan Church of Florence, and now archbishop of the same see, to write the history of the Vatican Council. All authentic documents relating to it were put into his hands. The first volume, entitled *Storia del Concilio Ecumenico Vaticano scritta sui Documenti Originali*, has been published. It extends over the period from the first conception of convoking an Œcumenical Synod to the close of the preparations for its work. I propose to give a condensed account of this first period, following closely the text of the Archbishop of Florence, and of the documents printed in the appendix to his work. I cannot omit to commend this volume to all who appreciate the purity of the *lingua Toscana*, of which it is a rare example. Its simplicity and transparent purity belong to the classical period of the Italian language.

It was on the 6th of December 1864, that Pius the Ninth for the first time manifested his thoughts on the convoking of an Œcumenical Council. He was presiding in the Vatican Palace over a session of the Congregation of Rites, consisting of cardinals and officials. After the usual prayer by which all such sessions are opened, the officials were bid to go out. For some time the Pope and the cardinals remained alone. The officials were then re-admitted, and the business of the congregation was despatched. This unusual event caused both surprise and curiosity.

Pius the Ninth, in that short interval, had made known to the cardinals that for a long time the thought of convoking an Œcumenical Council as an extraordinary remedy to the extraordinary needs of the Christian world had been before his mind. He bade the cardinals to weigh the matter each one by himself, and to communicate to him in writing, and separately, what before God they judged to be right. But he imposed rigorous silence upon them all.

This was the first conception of the Vatican Council.

The duty of weighing and delivering a written and separate opinion on the subject of convoking an Œcumenical Council was thus imposed on all cardinals then in Rome.

In the course of two months fifteen written opinions were delivered in. Others soon followed, until the number reached twenty-one.

The Archbishop of Florence, after a careful study of all these documents, has analysed and distributed the matter of them into the following heads. They treat of—

1. The present state of the world.
2. The question whether the state of the world requires the supreme remedy of an Œcumenical Council.

3. The difficulties of holding an Œcumenical Council, and how to overcome them.

4. The subjects which ought to be treated by such a Council.

(1.) In describing the present state of the world no reference was made by the Cardinals to its material progress in science, arts, or wealth, but to subjects strictly in relation to the eternal end of our existence. Under this aspect it is affirmed in these answers that the special character of this age is the tendency of a dominant party of men to destroy all the ancient Christian institutions, the life of which consists in a supernatural principle, and to erect upon their ruins and with their remains a new order, founded on natural reason alone. This tendency springs from two errors—the one that society, as such, has no duties towards God, religion being an affair of the individual conscience only; the other that the human reason is sufficient to itself, and that a supernatural order, by which man is elevated to a higher knowledge and destiny, either does not exist, or is at least beyond the cognisance and care of civil society. From these principles follows, by direct consequence, the exclusion of the Church and of revelation from the sphere of civil society and of science; and, further, out of this withdrawal of civil society and of science from the authority of revelation spring the Naturalism, Rationalism,

Pantheism, Socialism, Communism of these times. From these speculative errors flows in practice the modern revolutionary Liberalism, which consists in the assertion of the supremacy of the State over the spiritual jurisdiction of the Church, over education, marriage, consecrated property, and the temporal power of the head of the Church. This Liberalism, again, results in the indifferentism which equalises all religions, and gives equal rights to truth and error. The Consultors also treat of freemasonry, which substitutes for the Church of God a Universal Church of Humanity.

They then go on to speak of the infiltration of rationalistic principles into the philosophy of certain Catholic schools, and of their attitude of opposition to the divine authority of the Church. From this they pass to the internal state of the Church; to its discipline, which, since the Council of Trent, has become in many things inapplicable to the changed conditions of the world. Finally, they treat of the education of the clergy, the discipline of the monastic orders, and the disregard of the ecclesiastical laws by the laity in many countries.

(2.) For these and the like reasons almost all the cardinals were of opinion that the remedy of an Œcumenical Council was necessary—that is, to use the language of the schools, by a relative, not an absolute necessity. They say that though Luther was condemned by the pontiffs, the Council of Trent was thought to be necessary to give greater weight and solemnity to the condemnation. So also, though Pius the Ninth had condemned a long series of errors, it was expedient that the condemnation should be reported and published with the united voice of the whole episcopate joined to its head. They expressed the hope that if the whole Catholic episcopate in Council assembled should point out to the peoples and sovereigns of the Christian world the true relations of the natural and supernatural orders, the rights and the duties of the governors and the governed, it might serve to guide them in the confusion and obscurity which reign over the political order in this age of revolutions.

Only two cardinals out of twenty-one thought an Œcumenical Council not to be required—the one being of opinion that Councils are to be called only when some grave peril to the faith exists ; the other that the subjects to be treated were of too delicate a nature, and that the external helps needed for the celebraton of a Council did not now exist.

One also declined to give an opinion, referring himself to the judgment of the Supreme Pontiff.

Four, who thought a Council to be the remedy required by the evils of these times, nevertheless doubted if the moment were opportune, but still they admitted that, at least, all necessary preparations should be made for its convocation.

(3.) The Consultors then enumerated the obstacles in the way of holding a Council:—the confusions and disorders of the times; the animosity of the unbelieving and the profane, who would neither respect the authority of the Council nor fail to make pretexts out of its acts for attacking it more bitterly; the attitude of all civil governments, which are either hostile or indifferent; the probability of European war which would disperse or endanger the Council. Then again they suggest the difficulties internal to the Church; the absence of bishops from their dioceses; the danger that dissensions and parties might arise in the Council itself, and thereby divide the unity of the Catholic episcopate—a danger common to all times, but especially to these in which the subjects of possible divergence are so delicate and so wide-spread in their consequences. These reasons made some hesitate, and some pronounce against the holding of the Council. And even the majority who advised its convocation were fully aware of these opposing reasons, and did not deny their great weight.

Nevertheless they were of opinion that the need that a Council should be held was greater than the dangers of holding it. They believed that, grave as are the political and religious confusions, higher and nobler aspirations are not extinct; that a tendency to return towards the order of divine and supernatural truth is to be seen not only in individuals, but in the masses; that among the Catholic peoples a new life has sprung up, a great return of fervour, and an outspoken resistance to erroneous doctrines. They thought, therefore, that a Council would encourage and consolidate the faithful and fervent members of the Church, and, by its witness for truth, weaken the pretensions of those who oppose it; that the world could not do more against the Church after the Council than before it; that the Council of Nicæa was held in the face of the Arian contentions, and the Council of Trent when the north of Europe was on the verge of schism; that difficulties and dangers and the opposition of civil powers since the fourth century have threatened all Councils, but that Councils have always done their work which remains to this day. They said, too, that the great and lasting good gained by the Council for the whole Church would more than outweigh any harm from the temporary absence of bishops from their dioceses; and, finally, that if there should be dissensions and parties, so there were at Trent, but that when the Council had made its final decrees all returned to submission and concord. So it would be in the future Council.

One of the cardinals wrote as follows:

In these great affairs of the Church, they who have to treat them ought to rise high above those who are busied in politics. Men of the world trust in subtleties, astuteness, duplicities, and in means and views purely human. They who rule the Church trust in the prudence of the Gospel, in the truth, in the discharge of their own duties, and in the special assistance promised to the Church by its Divine Founder. Therefore it is that oftentimes what appears to be imprudent in the eye of those who go by human prudence alone is an act of evangelical prudence, and is both good and a duty, as well as an act of Divine Providence.

Another writes:

I see that whensoever the Church has deliberated about holding an Œcumenical Council, there were difficulties to surmount not less than those of to-day, and that if Divine Providence not only overcame them, but made them to turn to the greater good of the Church, so assuredly this assistance of the Holy Spirit, who *sweetly and mightily orders all things*, will not be wanting in a time when so many reasons concur to show the opportuneness of the same remedy, which, in all times whensoever it has been applied, has always produced the happiest and most imposing effects.

A third said:

God, who has suggested to your Holiness the thought of an Œcumenical Council to raise a strong defence against the vast evils of our time, will make the way plain, overcome all the difficulties, and give to your Holiness and to the bishops a moment of truce; peace, and time enough to fulfil so great a work.

(4.) The last point of consultation was of the matters to be treated. The Consultors first suggest the condemnation of modern errors, the exposition of

Catholic doctrine, the observance of discipline, its adaptation to the needs of the present time, and the raising of the state of the clergy and of the religious orders. Some of the cardinals touched upon special points, such as the licence of the press, the secret societies, civil marriage, the impediments to marriage, mixed marriages, ecclesiastical possessions, the observance of the feasts, abstinence, fasting, and the like. Two only spoke of the infallibility of the Pontiff: one of these spoke in general of Gallicanism. A third spoke also of Gallicanism, and of the present necessity of the temporal power of the Roman Pontiff in order to a free exercise of his ecclesiastical office. But this Consultor was one who opposed the holding of the Council. A fourth mentioned the temporal power. One only spoke of the syllabus, and he also was opposed to the holding of the Council. The Archbishop of Florence then goes on as follows:

> Certainly we must say that if the course of history does not prove that a pretended Jesuitical conspiracy controlled the programme of the Council, the cause of those who tell us, *usque ad nauseam*, that " Rome, by hidden schemes of that celebrated society, conceived the design of concentrating all power, ecclesiastical and civil, in the hands of the Supreme Pontiff, and setting up in the Church a new and exorbitant authority by the servility of the bishops," will be irreparably lost.[*]

Other points were touched upon by the cardinals. Many expressed their ardent desire that our brethren

[*] Cecconi, lib. i. c. i. p. 17.

separated from the Catholic Church might through the work of the Council find a way of return to the true mother of all the children of God.

II. After such full and careful deliberation, many might expect that Pius the Ninth would have proceeded to decide upon the convocation of the Council of the Vatican. Indeed, many have said that he was so strongly bent upon it, for the special purpose of his own "apotheosis," that he waited for no consultation, and endured no advice. History tells another tale. All that had hitherto been done was no more than a preliminary deliberation; and that only as to whether the subject of holding an Œcumenical Council should be so much as proposed for further deliberation.

In the first days of March 1865, Pius the Ninth directed certain of the cardinals to meet and confer together, by way of a preliminary discussion, on the very question whether an Œcumenical Council should be convoked or not. He ordered, likewise, that the written *voti*, or judgments of the Consultors, of which account has been already given, should be reduced to a compendium for the use of the new commission. This was done by the Procurator-General of the Dominican Order, in a brief form, under the title "Sketch of the Opinions expressed by the Cardinals invited by Pius the Ninth to advise on the Convocation of an Œcumenical Council." The compendium begins as follows: "The cardinals, to the number of thirteen, advised affirmatively for the convoking of a Council; one answered negatively, submitting his judgment to that of the Holy Father; one other concluded that a Council ought not to be convoked." The new commission then was composed of the Cardinals Patrizi, Reisach, Panebianco, Bizzarri, and Caterini.

The secretary of the commission was the Archbishop of Sardis, now Cardinal Giannelli, then Secretary of the Congregation of the Council, that is, for the interpretation of the Council of Trent and of all similar questions.

The first session was held on the 9th of March 1865, and the Consultors proceeded to re-examine the four heads, of which a hasty sketch has been already given.

The compendium was then subjected to a new and rigorous examination; and under the first head came the question of the necessity of Councils. It has been already said that the holding of Councils is not of absolute but only of relative necessity for the government of the Church. The meaning of this judgment is as follows. There is no divine commandment, no divine obligation, requiring that the bishops of the Universal Church should meet in one place. The government of the Church is adequately provided for in the divine institution of the Primacy and of the Episcopate. Nevertheless, for a multitude of reasons, both of natural and supernatural prudence, the Church, following the example of the Apostles, has always held not only diocesan and provincial synods, but also Œcumenical Councils.

For the first three hundred years no General Council was convened; for the last three hundred years no General Council has been summoned. For eighteen centuries, before 1869, only eighteen Councils had been held. General Councils, therefore, though useful and sometimes necessary, relatively to particular errors or particular times, are not absolutely necessary to the office of the Church. The Church is not infallible by reason of General Councils, but General Councils are infallible by reason of the Church. The Church does not depend on General Councils for the knowledge of the truth. Councils meet to give to truth, already known by divine tradition, a more precise expression for common and universal use. The whole Church, both the *Ecclesia docens* and the *Ecclesia discens*—that is, pastors in teaching, and the flock in believing—diffused throughout the world, is guided and kept in the way of truth at all times. The Church discharges its office as witness, judge and teacher, always and in all places. The Primacy in Rome and the Episcopate throughout the world, by the assistance of the Spirit of Truth abiding with it for ever, can never err in guarding and declaring the divine tradition of revelation. In the three hundred years before the Council of Nicæa, the living voice of the Church sufficed for the promulgation and diffusion of the faith; in the intervals between Council and Council the voice of the Church was sufficient in its declarations of truth and its condemnation of error. In the three hundred years since the Council of Trent, the Church has taught with the same divine and unerring authority. If it be asked, then, what need there can be for an Œcumenical Council, the answer is, that in applying remedies to the evils of the whole world, a knowledge of these wide-spread evils is necessary. More is seen by a multitude of eyes, and heard by a multitude of ears. The collective intelligence, culture, experience, instincts, and discernment, natural and supernatural, of the Episcopate, is the highest light of council upon earth. Such is the meaning of the words that the holding of Councils is not absolutely but relatively necessary.*

As to the obstacles in the way of holding the Council, the first was a doubt as to the disposition of the civil powers to permit the bishops of their respective jurisdictions to attend. Fear was especially entertained on this point in respect to the govern-

* *Petri Privilegium*, part i., pp. 76-81. Longmans.

ments of France, Italy, and Portugal. It was remembered that in 1862 the government of Italy hindered the Italian bishops from coming to Rome for the canonisation of the martyrs of Japan. But if the governments of Germany, Spain, Belgium, Holland, England, and America should put no hindrance, it was certain that a sufficient number of bishops would obey the call of the Supreme Pontiff.

As to the course to be pursued towards the sovereigns and civil powers, it was known that in all times, in convening Œcumenical Councils, the Church has endeavoured to act in accordance with Catholic sovereigns. This procedure was always held to be both fitting and useful, though not of necessity. Paul the Third, in convoking the Council of Trent, sought to obtain not only the assent of sovereigns, but their presence. In the bull of convocation he says:—"We asked the opinion of the princes, as it seemed to us that their assent to such an undertaking was above all expedient and opportune." And afterwards he adds:—"We urgently invited the Catholic sovereigns to come to the Council, and to bring with them the prelates of their respective countries." But he found the sovereigns undecided; and therefore, after many ineffectual attempts, he resolved to convoke the Council.

We desired (he said) to effect this object in accordance with and by the good-will of the princes of Christendom. But while we were waiting on their will, and looking for the time appointed by Thy will, O God, we felt ourselves at last impelled to declare that all times are surely acceptable to God, in which deliberation is taken in respect to things that are sacred and pertaining to Christian piety. Wherefore seeing, to our immeasurable sorrow, the Christian world daily growing worse, Hungary trodden down by the Turks, the Germans in peril, all other peoples afflicted with fear and grief, we had decided to wait no longer for the assent of any prince, nor to look to anything but to the will of Almighty God, and to the welfare of the Christian commonwealth.*

It was therefore thought fit that the Catholic sovereigns should be invited to appear by their legates at the Council of the Vatican, "according to the usage of the Church and the precedent of the Council of Trent."

Next it was proposed to call certain ecclesiastical persons from all parts of the world for previous consultation, inasmuch as "the benefit of the Council consists for the most part in knowing the state of the various regions and the remedies which there exist."

Finally, the Consultors recommended that all matters to be treated should be fully prepared and set in order before the assembling of the bishops, not only to avoid loss of time, but above all to preclude wandering discussions, and uncertainties of procedure, and the multiplication of innumerable questions.

* Bulla Pauli III. *Initia nostri*.

When the commission came to deliberate upon the likelihood of the Council being interrupted, dispersed, or suspended by reason of the state of Europe, they carefully reviewed the history of the Council of Trent, which was convoked in 1536 to meet at Mantua in May of the following year. It was then, by reason of opposition, prorogued till November 1537. Then it was deferred till May 1538, to meet at Vicenza. So few bishops came, by reason of war and of the disturbed state of Europe and of Italy, that the Pope, weary of proroguing, suspended the Council indefinitely. The Turks were still victorious, and Germany was every day losing its faith. Paul the Third, therefore, without asking the assent of princes, convoked the Council to meet in November 1542 in the city of Trent. Three legates went to Trent, and waited many months for the bishops, who were still unable to assemble by reason of war and the dangers of travel. The Council was again suspended till a more favourable time. After three years it was again fixed for March 1545. After this came another delay; and the Council opened in April following. After fifteen months it was transferred to Bologna, where the bishops were so few that no decree was made; and after five months it was again indefinitely prorogued.

It then remained suspended for four years. Under

Julius the Third it began once more in Trent in May 1551. It sat for a year; then in April 1552 it was suspended for two years, but the tumults of the world were such that it remained suspended for ten. In January 1562 it was opened again. In December 1563 the First Legate dismissed the bishops to their homes; and in January 1564 Pius the Fourth, by the bull *Benedictus Deus*, confirmed the work of the Council of Trent.

Such were the fortunes of the Council of Trent, without doubt the most momentous and fruitful Council of the Church in modern history. For three hundred years it has governed the Church throughout the world. And yet it could not meet till ten years after its convocation; twice it was suspended for two and for ten years; in eighteen years it was at work only five, in the midst of universal conflict. Its enemies might well deride its delays, prorogations, suspensions, and wanderings from city to city. But it did its work. All these facts were weighed in the first deliberation whether, in the uncertainties of our times, an Œcumenical Council could be held.

The commission then took, in order, the following questions:—

1. Whether the convoking of an Œcumenical Council was relatively necessary and opportune.

2. Whether a previous communication should be made to the Catholic princes.

3. Whether, before publishing the bull for convoking the Council, the Sacred College ought to be consulted, and how it should be done.

4. Whether it was opportune to form an extraordinary congregation, which should occupy itself with the direction of matters concerning the Council.

5. Whether the aforenamed congregation, which should take the name of Congregation of Direction, ought, after the publication of the bull, at once to consult certain bishops of various nations, that they might point out in a summary way the matters, whether of doctrine or of discipline, which they might think it opportune for the Council to treat, regard being had to the needs of their respective countries.

To these questions the five cardinals answered in the following way :—

To the first, the fourth, and the fifth affirmatively.

To the second negatively. But they added that it was nevertheless good and convenient that, at the time of publishing the bull, such steps as were opportune should be taken by the Holy See in respect to the Catholic princes.

To the third they answered affirmatively, but they added that it belonged to the Pope to decide in what way the Sacred College should be consulted.

As to the reference to the Catholic sovereigns, it is to be remembered that if certain sovereigns at this day continue to be Catholic, it is as individuals, not as sovereigns. The governments are not Catholic. The concordats which bound them to the Holy See have been abolished, not by the Holy See, but by their own revolutions, or by their legislatures, or by their liberal parties. Catholic sovereigns, therefore, no longer represent Catholic kingdoms; they have declared their states as such to have no religion, and have withdrawn their public laws from the unity of the Church and faith, and from obedience to the Holy See. To invite them to sit in an Œcumenical Council would be like inviting the public authorities of the United States to sit in the British Parliament.

The Consultors then requested one of their number to draw up an outline of the organisation whereby the matters to be treated would be subdivided and prepared with the greatest precision. These resolutions of the commission were reported by the secretary to Pius the Ninth, who approved them with one modification in the fifth question. He ordered that the reference to the bishops should be made before the publication of the bull of indiction.

The Commission of Direction was then formally instituted, comprising the five cardinals already named and certain others. Afterwards were added theologians and canonists selected in Rome and from other nations.

The following distribution was made of the subjects to be prepared :—1. Doctrine ; 2. Politico-Ecclesiastical or Mixed Questions; 3. Missions and the Oriental Churches ; 4. Discipline.

The affairs of the Holy See are committed to various "Congregations," or, as we should say, Departments of government, namely: The Holy Office, which deals with matters of faith; the Congregation of Propaganda, which directs the Church in all countries of which the sovereigns or governments are not Catholic; the Congregation of Extraordinary Ecclesiastical Affairs, which deals with all mixed questions in the relations of the spiritual and civil powers; the Congregation of Bishops and Regulars, which treats all questions of external jurisdiction ; the Congregation of the Council, instituted by Pius the Fourth at the instance of St Charles Borromeo for the interpretation of the decrees of the Council of Trent.

Now it was wisely determined, in accordance with the judgment of the commission, that the sections of the Congregation of Direction should each be, as it were, engrafted on the departments with which they had affinity.

The Congregation of Direction was therefore

divided into four Sections. The section of Doctrine had for its centre the Holy Office; that of the Mixed Questions, political and ecclesiastical, the Congregation of Ecclesiastical Affairs; that of Missions, the Congregation of Propaganda; and that of Discipline was attached to the Congregation of Bishops and Regulars, with the Congregation of the Council described before.

The object of this was to engraft these new consultative sections upon the departments in which the traditions of the Holy See and the maturest learning and experience in each separate matter are incorporated by immemorial usage. The special labours of these sections were to be afterwards laid before the entire Congregation of Direction. These minute details are given in order to show with what extreme and vigilant care the work of the Council was provided for. Nothing that human diligence could devise was omitted.

III. Thus far we have seen with what deliberation Pius the Ninth called to his Council the cardinals, theologians, and canonists of the Church in Rome. To these he proceeded also to add theologians and canonists from other nations to elaborate with prolonged examination, as we shall hereafter see, every part of the subject-matter to be proposed in the Council of the Vatican.

But even this was not deemed to be sufficient. The Pope then gave a further order that a circular letter should be sent to a number of the bishops of all nations, selected for their knowledge in theology and canon law and for their experience in the government of the Church. In this Pius the Ninth called to his aid those who were set as doctors by Christ Himself to teach the Church of God. Every bishop is, in virtue of his office, a doctor or teacher of the faith. It matters not how large or how small his diocese may be, whether it be in the Catholic unity or *in partibus infidelium*, whether he have a flock under his jurisdiction or not. The bishop of the least see in this is equal to the bishop of the greatest. He has been constituted a guardian of the faith by a divine commission, and his testimony as a witness is not greater or less in weight because the city over which he rules is greater or less in magnitude. It is the same in all. St Jerome says that in this all bishops are equal, and that the episcopate of the Bishop of Rome is no greater than that of the Bishop of Eugubium. We shall hereafter see the value and application of this principle.

This order was made in the audience given by Pius the Ninth to the secretary of the Congregation of Direction on the 27th of March 1865. Letters, under strict secret, were at once written to bishops selected from various parts of Europe, enjoining them to send in writing an enumeration of the subjects which they thought the Council ought to treat. These letters were addressed on the 10th of April to thirty-six bishops. Letters of like tenor were then despatched to certain bishops of the Oriental Churches. The answers were all returned to Rome by the month of August.

Although the injunction contained in the letters regarded only the matters to be treated, yet the bishops, in their replies, could not refrain from expressing their joy that the Pope had decided to hold an Œcumenical Council. The letters exhibit a wonderful harmony of judgment. They differ, indeed, in the degree of conciseness or diffuseness with which the several subjects are treated; but in the matters suggested for treatment they manifest the unanimity which springs from the unity of the Catholic episcopate.

The bishops note that in our time there exists no new or special heresy in matters of faith, but rather a universal perversion and confusion of first truths and principles which assail the foundations of truth and the preambles of all belief. That is to say, as doubt attacked faith, unbelief has avenged faith by destroying doubt. Men cease to doubt when they disbelieve outright. They have come to deny that the light of nature and the evidences of creation prove the existence of God. They deny, therefore, the existence of God, the existence of the soul, the dictates of conscience, of right and wrong, and of the moral law. If there be no God, there is no legislator, and their morality is independent of any lawgiver, and exists in and by itself, or rather has no existence except subjectively in individuals, by customs inherited from the conventional use and the mental habits of society. They note the wide-spread denial of any supernatural order, and therefore of the existence of faith. They refer to the assertion that science is the only truth which is positive, and to the alleged sufficiency of the human reason for the life and destinies of man, or, in other words, deism, independent morality, secularism, and rationalism, which have invaded every country of the west of Europe. The bishops suggest that the Council should declare that the existence of God may be certainly known by the light of nature, and define the natural and supernatural condition of man, redemption, grace, and the Church. They specially desired the treatment of the nature and personality of God distinct from the world, creation, and providence, the possibility and the fact of a divine revelation. These points may seem strange to many readers, but those who know the philosophies current in Germany and France will at once perceive the wisdom of these suggestions.

They then more explicitly propose for treatment the elevation of man by grace at creation to a superior natural order, the fall of man, his restoration in Christ, the divine institution of the Church, the mission entrusted to it by its Divine Founder, its organization, its endowments and rights, the primacy, and the jurisdiction of the Roman Pontiff; its independence of civil powers, and its relation to them; its authority over education, and the present necessity of the temporal power of the Holy See. These points have been here recited in full in order to show that the one subject for which, we are told, the Council was assembled, was hardly so much as mentioned. Out of thirty-six bishops a few only suggested the infallibility of the head of the Church, though his primacy could not be treated without it.

> They are very few (writes one of the bishops) who at this day impugn this prerogative of the Roman Pontiff; and this they do, not in virtue of theological reasons, but with the intention of affirming the liberty of science with greater safety. It seems that with this view a school of theologians has sprung up in Bavaria, at Munich, who in all their writings have principally before them, by the help of historical dissertations, to lower the Apostolic see, its authority, and its mode of government, by throwing contempt upon it, and by attacking, above all, the infallibility of Peter teaching *ex cathedrâ*.

With these few exceptions the bishops occupied themselves with Pantheism, Rationalism, Naturalism, Socialism, Communism, indifference in matters of religion, Regalism, the licence of conscience and of the press, civil marriage, spiritism, magnetism, the false theories on inspiration, on the authority of Scripture, and on interpretation. Many of them refer to the syllabus as giving the best outline of matters to be treated, and express the desire that the errors therein condemned should be condemned in the Council, " non ut majori firmitate, sed ut majori solemnitate proscribantur." These points have been here recounted in order to show that what some persons would expect alone to find was hardly so much as named in the midst of an interminable list of subjects. It is needless to say that the doctrine of infallibility is not to be found in the syllabus, which consists of the condemnation of eighty errors classed under ten heads, namely: 1. Those that relate to the existence of God; 2. To revelation; 3. To indifferentism; 4. To Socialism; 5. To errors as to the Church and its rights; 6. To errors in respect to politics and the State; 7. To errors as to natural and Christian morality; 8. To errors respecting Christian marriage; 9. To errors respecting the temporal power of the Roman Pontiff; 10. To the errors of modern liberalism. Once more, this outline of the syllabus is given because it may well be believed that of the thousands who denounce it few have read it. If they would read it, they would be not a little astonished to find that, with few exceptions, any sincere believer in Christian revelation would condemn as erroneous what is condemned in the syllabus.

"The theories of Naturalism," said one of the bishops, "have introduced into modern society habits altogether sensual and material, far removed from the Christian life." He hoped that the Council would go into details of practice, and condemn the excess of luxury, the indecent amusements, the haste to get rich by speculations of questionable honesty, the abandonment of domestic life, the profanation of marriage, the disregard of the days consecrated to God's service, the neglect of divine worship, the practices of usury. They further asked for a *catechismus ad populum*, as the Council of Trent ordered a *catechismus ad parochos*. They desired, further, a new code or digest of the canon law, from which should be excluded all that is obsolete and, by reason of the transformation of modern society, no longer expedient or of possible observance.

They desired also that the relations between the Church and State, or the spiritual and civil powers, might be clearly defined. They asked that broad and intelligible principles might be laid down from which they could never depart in judging of these mixed questions ; that the Council would define in what way they ought to comport themselves in the presence of such facts as the civil liberty of the press and of worship, and of the protection which governments afford to error. They desired especially that the Council should make some declaration on the imminent danger of Christian governments lapsing into the tyranny of a pagan Cæsarism, by which the state is deified, and all that is called God or worshipped is included in the sphere of its arbitrary power.

Lastly, they desired that the Council should declare that the temporal power of the Pontiff is no obstacle to any progress founded upon the laws of the Christian world; that the unhappy conflict between the spiritual and civil powers which now convulses the world arose not from any aggression on the part of the Church, but from the departure of modern civilisation from the basis of Christian society. The last error condemned in the syllabus is that "the Roman Pontiff can and ought to reconcile himself and come to terms with progress, liberalism, and modern civilisation." The Christian civilisation represented by the Roman Pontiff consists in the unity of faith, the unity of worship, of Christian marriage and Christian education. No reasonable man can wonder, therefore, if Pius the Ninth declines to reconcile himself with indifferentism in faith and worship, divorce courts, and secular schools.

We may now sum up this part of our subject which carries us down to the first public announcement of the intention to convoke the Council of the Vatican.

It will be seen that the initiative was altogether by the act of Pius the Ninth. He was the first to conceive and to lay open this thought to his legitimate counsellors. Moreover, we have the declared motive of his thought. It was "to find an extraordinary remedy for the extraordinary evils of the Christian world." We have seen also that in the deliberate answers of the cardinals and of the bishops the same is the governing thought. The evils of the modern world, its theological, philosophical, religious, social, domestic, and moral confusions, these so filled the mind of the Pontiff and his counsellors that what the world has been taught to believe was the chief if not the only motive for holding the Council hardly appears; and when it appears it is either enumerated in a series of doctrines of which each demands the other, or it is suggested by one of the cardinals who opposed the holding of a Council altogether.

The true motive of the Vatican Council is transparent to all calm and just minds. For three hundred years no General Council had been held, for three hundred years the greatest change that has ever come upon the world since its conversion to Christianity had steadily passed upon it. The first period of the Church gradually brought about the union of the spiritual and civil powers of the world in amity and co-operation. The last three hundred years have parted and opposed them to each other. The mission of the Apostles in the beginning united men of all nations, and therefore, in prelude, all nations, in one spiritual society. The events of these last times have withdrawn the nations as political bodies from the unity of the faith. In the second period, or the middle age of the Christian world, how frequent and great soever the conflicts between the spiritual and civil powers might be, nevertheless the public life, and laws, and living organisation of Christendom were Christian. Princes and legislatures and society professed the Catholic faith, and were subject to the head of the Catholic Church. Christendom was one in faith, one in worship, under one supreme pastor; its marriage law and its education were alike Christian.

A writer of much authority in English literature has said that the first French Revolution was the last act of the Lutheran reformation. What his own interpretation of these words may be it is not for others to say. Perhaps it may be that the individuality of private judgment in religion passed in 1789 into the domain of politics, and that the critical spirit which has dissolved positive faith has disintegrated also the authority of governments. Political writers have been telling us that the governments of the west of Europe are visibly weak—indeed, that they seem to have lost the skill or the power of government—and that they have become simply the index of the changes of the popular will, which veers and travels throughout the whole cycle of the compass with the rapidity of wind. Another obvious interpretation of this dictum is that the first national separation from the unity of Christendom was effected by Luther. The conflicts of nations during what was called the Great Western Schism, the separate and antagonistic obediences which for a time divided the nations, all based and defended themselves on the principle of unity which they claimed each one for their own section. But all these separations were once more reunited in the Council of Constance. The separations of the sixteenth century were not of this sort. They were the formal going out of nations from the world-wide family of Christendom, based and defended upon the principle that participation in the unity of the Catholic Church was not necessary, and that every nation contained within itself the fountain of faith and of jurisdiction, and being independent of all authority external to itself, was therefore self-sufficing. From this followed legitimately the attempt to transfer to the crown the jurisdiction of the spiritual head of the Christian Church. It has been truly said that the royal supremacy is pregnant with negation. It denies and excludes the action of the Catholic Church throughout the world from any nation in which the sovereign is over all causes, ecclesiastical and civil, supreme. In Germany, Sweden, Denmark, England, the Lutheran supremacy of the crown was fully established, with what results the state of those countries at this day attests. But it was not on them that Pius the Ninth primarily and chiefly fixed his eyes. His chief care was for the Catholic kingdoms of Europe, in which the Lutheran Reformation has never established itself. Nevertheless, in them regalism, which is a royal supremacy pushed to the very verge of schism, has universally prevailed. In France from Louis the Fourteenth to the other day, in Austria from Joseph the Second, in Tuscany from Leopold the First, in Spain from Charles the Third, in Naples from the beginning of the *Sicilian monarchy*, the royal power has oppressed and enslaved the Church with its fatal fostering protection. Constantine called himself only ἐπίσκοπος τῶν ἔξω. But the Catholic sovereigns of the last three centuries have meddled internally in everything, from the nomination of bishops to the number of candles to be lighted upon the altar. Frederick of Prussia used to call Joseph of Austria "mon frère le sacristan." The consequences of this disastrous patronage were manifold, and ramified throughout the whole organisation of the Church. It will be enough to name three: first, the lowering and secularising of the episcopate and priesthood by contact with courts and their ambitions; secondly, the suspension of the spiritual liberty of the Church in its discipline, synods, and tribunals; and, thirdly, the protection given by kings to unsound teachers, as Van Espen, de Hontheim in canon law, and in theology to the authors of the Four Articles, by Louis the Fourteenth. In this sense it is most true that the Lutheran movement has steadily penetrated into Catholic countries. This excessive regalism produced its inevitable reaction, and the revolutions of this century have paralysed all royal supremacies by establishing the doctrine that the State, as such, has no religion.

It may therefore be said that the second period of the Christian world has closed. Of thirty-six crowned heads ten are still Catholic, two are of the Greek separation, twenty-four are nominally Protestant. The people of many and great nations are faithful and fervent children of the Catholic Church, but the Revolution either openly or secretly, in its substance or in its spirit, is behind every throne and in almost every government and legislature of the Christian world. The public laws even of the nations in which the people are Catholic are Catholic no longer. The unity of the nations in faith and worship, as the Apostles founded it, seems now to be dissolved. The unity of the Church is more compact and solid than ever, but the Christendom of Christian kingdoms is of the past. We have entered into a third period. The Church began not with kings, but with the peoples of the world, and to the peoples, it may be, the Church will once more return. The princes and governments and legislatures of the world were everywhere against it at its outset: they are so again. But the hostility of the nineteenth century is keener than the hostility of the first. Then the world had never believed in Christianity; now it is falling from it. But the Church is the same, and can renew its relations with whatsoever forms of civil life the world is pleased to fashion for itself. If, as political foresight has predicted, all nations are on their way to democracy, the Church will know how to meet this new and strange aspect of the world. The high policy of wisdom by which the Pontiffs held together the dynasties of the Middle Age will know how to hold together the peoples who still believe. Such was the world on which Pius the Ninth was looking out when he conceived the thought of an Œcumenical Council. He saw the world which was once all Catholic tossed and harassed by the revolt of its intellect against the revelation of God, and of its will against his law; by the revolt of civil society against the sovereignty of God; and by the anti-christian spirit which is driving on princes and governments towards anti-christian revolutions. He to whom, in the words of St John Chrysostom, the whole world was committed, saw in the Council of the Vatican the only adequate remedy for the world-wide evils of the nineteenth century.

It will be remembered that the Consultors, in giving their opinion that the holding of a Council was expedient, gave no opinion as to the time when it could safely be convoked. The threatening aspect of the times was enough to make them hesitate.

On the 17th of November 1865, letters were written to the nuncios at Paris, Vienna, Madrid, Munich, and Brussels, announcing the intention of Pius the Ninth to hold an Œcumenical Council, and desiring them to give their opinion whether the circumstances of the times were such as to make its convocation prudent. They were also directed to send the names of two theologians or canonists of special reputation in the respective countries to which they were accredited. Their answers came at the close of the year 1865.

The Commission of Direction held its third session

on the 24th of May 1866, but from that date till the middle of 1867 it did not meet again. This suspension in its preparations was caused by events which it may be well to enumerate. All Europe was anxiously awaiting the conflict between Prussia and Austria, which soon broke out and soon ended on the field of Sadowa. On the 17th of June, the King of Prussia declared war against the Emperor; and three days after Baron Ricasoli announced to the Chambers and the Senate that King Victor Emanuel had also declared war against Austria. Lombardy and Venice were ceded to Italy; and on the 4th of November Victor Emanuel, at Turin, announced that "Italy was made but not completed." On the 15th of September 1864, the Emperor of the French and the King of Italy had entered into a convention by which Italy bound itself not to attack the Pontifical States, and to defend them by force against any assailant, and France bound itself gradually to withdraw its troops within two years from Rome and the States of the Church. On the 11th of December 1866, the French flag was lowered on the Castle of St Angelo. Three days before, the French general in command had taken his leave of Pius the Ninth. In reply to his words of farewell, the Pope answered, "We must not deceive ourselves; the revolution will come here. It has proclaimed its intention, and you have heard it." On the following Christmas Day, in reply to the congratulations of the Sacred College, the Pope said: "Difficult and sorrowful are the days in which we live, but we ought, therefore, all the more to strengthen ourselves in the hope of greater help from the Almighty; and, whatsoever happens, we ought not to be afraid."* The condition of Europe at that time was thus described, on the 12th of November 1866, by an English hand:—

> The immediate consequence of the last war (between Prussia and Austria), and of the peace which followed it, was to break the old alliances, and to trouble every European State. The invasion of Denmark gave the first shock to public morality, and the subsequent quarrel between Prussia and Austria annihilated the barriers of international law. From henceforth there no longer exists a principle of general policy in Europe, and ambition has no limit to the extension of its own power. Every man's hand is against his brother, and only the necessity of defence hinders the desire of attack. All nations are on the watch, and order is maintained because everybody is afraid of his neighbour. The Continental press shows us one-half of Europe in array against the other. . . . The whole of Europe is arming. France does not disarm, but, on the contrary, increases its armies; Russia is raising three hundred thousand recruits; Prussia is reorganising four new army corps; Austria is remodelling and reforming its army; everywhere the armaments are in training, and new systems of warfare are being elaborated. The art of slaying threatens to become the sole industry of Europe.†

It is, therefore, no wonder that Pius the Ninth and his counsellors hesitated to fix the day for the open-

---

* Cecconi, lib. i., c. iv., note.   † *Times*, Nov. 12, 1866.

ing of the Council. The Pope had at one time thought of fixing the 29th of June in 1867, on which the eighteenth centenary of St Peter's martyrdom would fall; but the aspect of Europe, and the clouds which were visibly rolling towards the walls of Rome, caused him to pause. Therefore, on the 8th of December 1866, a circular letter was written to all the bishops of the Catholic Church, inviting them to Rome in the following year for the solemnities of the centenary alone, the importance of which no one at that time foresaw. But this must be narrated hereafter.

CHAPTER II.

THE CENTENARY OF ST PETER: AND PREPARATIONS FOR THE COUNCIL.

No one who has watched with any attention the pontificate of Pius the Ninth will believe that the definition of the infallibility of the Roman Pontiff was the work of any parties or intrigues. Faith may move mountains, but cliques and cabals are agencies too human and too narrow to move Œcumenical Councils. Not just men only, but thoughtful men, will seek for wider and more adequate causes of such effects. And such causes lie on the surface of the history of this pontificate.

I. 1. Before the Council of the Vatican assembled, Pius the Ninth had three times called the bishops of the Universal Church to Rome. In the year 1854, 206 cardinals and bishops assembled for the definition of the Immaculate Conception; in 1862, 265 bishops came for the canonisation of the martyrs of Japan; and now a third time 500 bishops assembled from all parts of the world to celebrate the eighteenth Centenary of St. Peter's martyrdom. No pontiff from the beginning, in all the previous successions of 256 popes, has ever so united the bishops with himself. Each of these three assemblies had a special significance. In 1854 the bishops assisted at the promulgation of a doctrine of faith by the sole authority of their head; in 1862 the bishops with an unanimous voice declared their belief that the temporal power or princedom of the Roman Pontiff is a dispensation of the providence of God, in order that the head of the Church may with independence and freedom exercise his spiritual primacy. In 1867, 500 bishops unanimously proclaimed their adhesion to the pontifical acts of Pius the Ninth, both in the teaching of truth and in the condemnation of errors—that is to say, to the syllabus then recently published, which is a compendium of the acts of Pius the Ninth in the many and important encyclicals and other letters of his pontificate promulgated before that date.

In these three assemblies at the Tomb of the Apostle and around the throne of his successor there was an explicit act of submission to his primacy, and a more than implicit confession of his infallibility.

2. It may be truly said that since the year 1854 the subject of the infallibility of the Roman Pontiff had been more than ever before the mind of the episcopate. If Pius the Ninth did not bear an infallible office, what was the act of 1854? The bishops who assembled at the definition of the Immaculate Con-

The True Story of the Vatican Council. 43

ception were not an Œcumenical Council, nor any council at all. They were not convened as a council. Pius the Ninth alone defined the Immaculate Conception. His act was, therefore, infallible or nothing. The world outside the Catholic Church no doubt accounted it to be nothing; but the whole episcopate and the whole Catholic unity accounted it to be infallible.

It is certain, then, that the events of 1854 powerfully awakened in the minds of both clergy and laity the thought of infallibility. In like manner the canonisation of 1862 elicited from the mind of the Church an express recognition of the prerogatives of the successor of Peter. For many years, by allocutions and apostolic letters, Pius the Ninth had been condemning the doctrines of philosophers and revolutionists. His supreme office as teacher of the Universal Church had been denied by those who endeavoured to restrict it to the dogmas of faith. In the midst of this continuous warfare, the bishops assembled in 1862, and addressed Pius the Ninth in these words:

> Long may you live, Holy Father, to rule the Catholic Church. Go onward, as now, in defending it with your power, guiding it with your prudence, adorning it with your virtues. Go before us, as the Good Shepherd, by your example; feed the sheep and the lambs with heavenly food; refresh them with the streams of heavenly wisdom. For you are to us the teacher of sound doctrine, the centre of unity, the unfailing light to the nations kindled by divine wisdom. You are the Rock, the foundation of the Church against which the gates of hell shall not prevail.

When you speak we hear Peter's voice, when you decide we obey the authority of Christ.*

There can be little discernment in any man who cannot perceive how these two events brought out the infallibility of the Roman Pontiff—that of 1854 in the defining of a dogma of faith, that of 1862 in matters which, though not dogmas of faith, are nevertheless in contact with his supreme office as "teacher of all Christians."

3. But, powerfully as these two events tended to bring before the minds of men the subject of the authority of the Pontiff as the successor of Peter, they bear no proportion in their power and efficacy to the Centenary of St. Peter's martyrdom in 1867. In the month of June in that year bishops from all parts of the world began to arrive in Rome. There were bishops who travelled from regions which lay far beyond any practicable road. Some came from the furthest East, others from the extreme West, some came from Africa, some from South America, some from Australia. Thirty nations were represented by their patriarchs, archbishops, primates, and bishops. All languages were to be heard, and all costumes were to be seen in the streets. It was said that the population of Rome was nearly doubled by the concourse of

---

* Declaration of the Bishops, June 8, 1862, in the "Acts of the Canonisation of the Martyrs of Japan," p. 543. Rome, 1864.

Catholics from all parts of the world. Now what was the motive of this assemblage? It was simply the faith that Pius the Ninth is successor of Peter and heir of all his primacy with all its prerogatives and gifts. Since the Council of Chalcedon and of the second of Lyons—for the number at the Lateran Council is doubtful—500 bishops had never assembled together: at Chalcedon, where they exclaimed "*Peter has spoken by Leo*," Leo was not there. But in Rome at this time Peter's successor was at their head. It was not only the festival of the martyrdom of Peter, but of his primacy over all the world. The bishops, when they met around his tomb in the great Basilica of Constantine, knew that they were making a profession of faith in the primary of his successor.

4. It does not belong to the story of the Vatican Council to describe the external ceremonial of the Centenary; but it does emphatically belong to the right appreciation of the acts of the Vatican Council that the bearing of the Centenary upon it should be fully understood. It is not too much to say that of the proximate causes of the definition of the infallibility, the Centenary of St Peter's martyrdom was the most powerful. And this, I hope, will be made clear by a simple narrative of facts.

The solemnities of the Centenary consisted in the following acts:—

First, in the Consistory of the 26th of June, at which five hundred bishops were present. The number being so great, it was held in the tribune over the atrium of St Peter's, where the *cœna* on Maunday Thursday used to be laid. It was in this consistory that Pius the Ninth for the first time publicly announced his intention of holding an Œcumenical Council.

Secondly came the festival of the Centenary. The Pope sung the first vespers of the Feast with great solemnity in St Peter's on the evening of the 28th; he sung also the pontifical mass on the following day at the high altar in the presence of half the bishops of the world.

Lastly, on the 1st of July the Holy Father gave audience to the bishops to receive from them their address or response to his allocution on the 26th.

Before we enter upon these events, it will be well to narrate one fact which throws much light upon the intention of Pius the Ninth in convoking the Council. The 17th of June was the anniversary of his creation. After mass in the Sistine Chapel, he went into the Pauline Chapel to unvest. The Cardinal Vicar, in the name of the Sacred College, made the usual address of congratulation, ending with the words that they wished to the Holy Father "health and many years to see the peace and triumph of the Church." The Pope answered in substance as follows:—

I accept your good wishes from my heart, but I remit their verification to the hand of God. We are in a moment of great crisis. If we look only to the aspect of human events, there is no hope; but we have a higher confidence. Men are intoxicated with dreams of unity and progress, but neither is possible without justice. Unity and progress based on pride and egotism are illusions. God has laid on me the duty to declare the truths on which Christian society is based, and to condemn the errors which undermine its foundation. And I have not been silent. In the encyclical of 1864, and in that which is called the Syllabus, I declared to the world the dangers which threaten society, and I condemned the falsehoods which assail its life. That act I now confirm in your presence, and I set it again before you as the rule of your teaching. To you, venerable brethren, as bishops of the Church, I now appeal to assist me in this conflict with error. On you I rely for support. I am aged and alone, praying on the mountain; and you, the bishops of the Church, are come to hold up my arms. The Church must suffer, but it will conquer. "Preach the word; be instant in season, out of season; reprove, entreat, rebuke, with all patience and doctrine." For there shall be a time—and that time is come —"when they will not endure sound doctrine." The world will contradict you, and turn from you; but be firm and faithful. "For I am even now ready to be sacrificed, and the time of my dissolution is at hand." "I have, I trust, 'fought a good fight,' and 'have kept the faith,' and there is laid up for you, and I hope for me also, 'a crown of justice which the Lord, the just Judge, will render to me at that day.'"*

5. If we look upon the Centenary only as a demonstration of moral power and of the superiority of the

* "Centenary of St Peter and the General Council," pp. 6, 7. Longmans.

moral over the material order of the world, it has a deep significance. Pius the Ninth was at that moment in the crisis to which the Italian revolution of so many years had been advancing. All protection of the Catholic powers of the world, of whom France had been till then the mandatory, had been withdrawn. He knew that the revolution would come to Rome again with more formidable power than in 1848. "Verrà fin qui," as he said in his farewell to the general of the French army. In the face of all menace, and with the certainty of the coming revolution, Pius the Ninth had the year before convened the Catholic episcopate to meet in Rome in 1867. No event, excepting the Council of the Vatican, has in our age manifested so visibly to the intellect and so palpably even to the sense of men the unity, universality, unanimity, and authority of the only Church which alone can endure St Augustine's two tests, *cathedra Petri* and *diffusa per orbem*— union with the See of Peter, and expansion throughout the world. The Centenary was a confession of faith, without an accent of controversy. Even those who were not of the unity of the Church recognised it as such. Whosoever believed in Christianity, and desired the spread of our Lord's kingdom upon earth, could not fail to see in that great gathering the wide foundations laid by the apostolic mission. Even they who reject certain Catholic doctrines hold the Creed of the Apostles, which has been guarded by the Catholic Church. Even they who rest their faith on Scriptures alone, still more they who rest it upon fathers and councils, know that the custody of all these is in the Church which assembled on that day round the centre of its unity. The world-wide Church is the great witness upon whose broad testimony all Christians must ultimately rest. Take the Catholic and Roman Church out of the world, and where is Christendom? These reasons moved even those who were not in the unity of the Church to a respectful silence. But if such was the undeniable action of the Centenary upon just and considerate men outside its unity, what was it upon those who were within? This we shall best show by quoting the words of Pius the Ninth in the allocution of the 26th of June, and the answer of the bishops in the audience of the 1st of July.

6. Pius the Ninth addressed the 500 bishops who had gathered round him from all parts of the world in these words:

> If the general good of the faithful be considered, what, venerable brethren, can be more timely and wholesome for Catholic nations, in order to increase their obedience towards us and the Apostolic See, than that they should see how highly the sanctity and the rights of Catholic unity are prized by their pastors, and should behold them, for that cause, traversing great distances

by sea and land, deterred by no difficulties from hastening to the Roman See, that they may pay reverence in the person of our humility to the successor of Peter and the vicar of Christ on earth? For by this authority of example, far better than by subtil doctrine, they will perceive what reverence, obedience, and submission they ought to bear towards us, to whom, in the person of Peter, Christ our Lord said, "Feed my lambs—feed my sheep," and in those words entrusted and committed to us the supreme care and power over the Universal Church.

For what else did Christ our Lord intend us to understand when He set Peter as head to defend the stability of his brethren, saying, "I have prayed for thee, that thy faith fail not?" He intended, as S. Leo implies, that "the Lord took a special care of Peter, and prayed expressly for Peter's faith, as if the state of the others would be more certain if the mind of their chief were unconquered. In Peter, therefore, the fortitude of all was guarded and the help of divine grace was so ordained that the stability which was given by Christ to Peter, by Peter should be bestowed on the rest of the apostles. Nay, venerable brethren, we have never doubted but that out of the very tomb where the ashes of blessed Peter rest for the perpetual veneration of the world, a secret power and healing virtue goes forth to inspire the pastors of the Lord's flock," &c.

To this the bishops unanimously answered:

We take part more fervently in the present celebration, as contemplating, in the solemnity which this day brings round again, the unshaken firmness of the Rock whereon our Lord and Saviour built His Church, solid and perpetual. For we perceive it to be an effect of the power of God, that the chair of Peter, the organ of truth, the centre of unity, the foundation and bulwark of the Church's freedom, should have stood firm and unmoved for now eighteen hundred years complete, amid so many adverse circumstances and such constant efforts of its enemies; that while kingdoms and empires rose and fell in turn, it should so have stood, as a secure beacon to direct men's course through the tempestuous sea of life, and show, by its light, the safe anchorage and harbour of salvation.

Five years ago we rendered our due testimony to the sublime office you bear, and gave public expression to our prayers for you, for your civil princedom, and the cause of right and of religion. We then professed, both in words and writing, that nothing was more true or dearer to us than to believe and teach those things which you believe and teach, than to reject those errors which you reject. All those things which we then declared we now renew and confirm. Never has your voice been silent. You have accounted it to belong to your supreme office to proclaim eternal verities, to smite the errors of the time which threaten to overthrow the natural and supernatural order of things and the very foundations of ecclesiastical and civil power. So that at length all may know what it is that every Catholic should hold, retain, and profess. Believing that Peter has spoken by the mouth of Pius, therefore whatsoever you have spoken, confirmed, and pronounced for the safe custody of the deposit, we likewise speak, confirm, and pronounce; and with one voice and one mind we reject everything which, as being opposed to divine faith, the salvation of souls, and the good of human society, you have judged fit to reprove and reject. For that is firmly and deeply established in our consciousness, which the fathers at Florence defined in their Decree on Union, that the Roman Pontiff "is the vicar of Christ, head of the whole Church, and father and teacher of all Christians; and that to him in the person of blessed Peter has been committed by our Lord Jesus Christ full power to feed, to rule, and to govern the Universal Church."[*]

The full meaning of this declaration of the bishops will not be understood unless we bear in mind that they were speaking of the doctrinal acts of Pius the Ninth during his pontificate, of which the definition

[*] "Petri Privilegium," part i. pp. 28—33. Longmans.

of the Immaculate Conception, the encyclical, and the syllabus were the most prominent and the most recent. We see, then, half the episcopate of the Church proclaiming that from the moment that the voice of Pius the Ninth reached them, all the declarations and condemnations of the successor of Peter were to them, not necessarily in all things matters of faith because the greater part of the syllabus is in matters not revealed, but the rule of their teaching. With what consistency or sincerity could this be said of any teacher for whose declarations and condemnations there was no special guidance and guarantee? Without doubt these words did not explicitly declare the Roman Pontiff to be infallible, but half the episcopate of the Church would be not unreasonably accused of great temerity in their language if they had not believed the head of the Church to be in some special way guarded from error in his teaching.

7. The address from which this passage is taken was prepared as follows. Nothing can more clearly show how consciously present to the mind of the bishops at that time was the infallibility of their head. A general meeting of bishops was convened at the Altieri Palace, to draw up an address in reply to the allocution of the Holy Father. Bishops of every nation were present, and it was found impossible to frame any document in so

numerous an assembly. It was therefore decided to entrust the drawing up of the address to a commission of seven—namely, the Cardinal De Angelis, Archbishop of Fermo, the Archbishops of Sorrento, Saragossa, Kalocsa, Thessalonica (now Cardinal Franchi), Westminster, and the Bishop of Orleans. At the first meeting of the commission it was agreed to entrust the preparing of the first draft of the address to Mgr. Haynald, the Archbishop of Kalocsa. At the next meeting of the commission the draft was examined. In outline it was nearly as it was adopted at last; but in one point, bearing intimately on the history of the Council, it underwent an important revision. As it originally stood, the word *infallible* was, in more places than one, ascribed to the office and authority of the Pontiff. To this word, as expressing a doctrine of Catholic truth, no member of the commission objected. It was however said that the word *infallible* had as yet been used only in provincial councils, or pastoral letters, or theological schools, but that it had not been inserted in the formal acts of any general council of the Church, and that, inasmuch as the 500 bishops then in Rome were not assembled in council, it might be advisable not to seem to assume the action or office of a Council. These considerations were assented to by all. It was then proposed to insert the words of the Council of

Florence, which was the last authoritative decree on the primacy of the Roman Pontiff. To this no objection as to the subject-matter was made; but it was urged that the draft address already contained expressions stronger than the decree of the Council of Florence, which only implicitly contains the infallibility of the head of the Church as the teacher of all Christians, for the address explicitly declares that "Peter has spoken by the mouth of Pius." To this it was answered that though beyond all doubt these words explicitly declare the voice of the Pontiff to be infallible as Peter was, yet this acclamation of the fathers of Chalcedon and that of the third Council of Constantinople were always, and not unreasonably, set aside as of little weight in controversy, as little more than rhetorical amplifications of the authority of Leo and of Agatho. They were not doctrinal formulas, much less definitions, but only acclamations; and acclamations define nothing, and can form neither objects of faith nor terminations of controversy. It was therefore by the vote of almost all the seven members of the commission, if not indeed by the united vote of all, decided that the words of the decree of the Florentine Council should be inserted. These facts are here noted in detail because their importance will be seen hereafter. They prove that at the Centenary in 1867 the primacy of the Roman

Pontiff, with its full prerogatives and endowments, was vividly before the minds of the bishops. The Centenary in itself, with all its solemnities, admonitions, and associations, threw out into visible and palpable relief the twofold office of the successor of Peter in doctrine and jurisdiction, or, in other words, his primacy and the divine assistance by which it is perpetually sustained in the custody of revealed truth. The facts prove also the circumspection with which the members of the commission avoided everything which could have the semblance of anticipating the action of the future Council, or of engaging the bishops by any expressions in any declaration beyond the previous and authoritative teaching of the Church. Nevertheless, there can be no doubt that the impression made by the Centenary upon the minds of the bishops determined many to promote, by all means in their power, the closing of a controversy which had for centuries periodically disturbed the Church.

8. It may not be out of place to give here an outline of the question of the infallibility—its origin, its climax, and its determination. But in writing the story of the Vatican Council it will be more fitting simply to trace the history of the question than to treat it theologically. A history is a narrative, not an argument, and the qualities required in a narrative

are truth and accuracy, not a polemical defence of the truths narrated. This belongs to the province of dogmatic theology.*

Like other contested doctrines of Christianity, the infallibility of the head of the Church has had three periods: the first was a period of simple belief, the second a period of analysis and controversy, the third a period of gradual determination and final definition. The doctrine of the Immaculate Conception is a fair example. It has visibly passed through these three stages. It was implicitly contained in the universal belief of the Church, both East and West, that the Blessed Virgin was a person without sin, and sanctified by a pre-eminent and exceptional sanctification. This was the first period of unanalysed belief. The second period began in the Pelagian controversy, when S. Augustin, in affirming the universality of original sin, expressly excepted the mother of our Lord. This exemption from original sin was analytically accounted for in two ways—either that she was liberated from it and born without it, or that she was always free from it in the first moment of her existence. The former is the doctrine of the Immaculate Nativity, the latter of the Immaculate Conception. The third period dates from the eleventh century,

* The theological argument may be found in the first and second parts of "Petri Privilegium." Longmans.

during which the doctrine of the Immaculate Nativity was seen to be less and less adequate to explain the absolute sinlessness of the mother of our Redeemer, and the doctrine of the Immaculate Conception was seen to be more and more in conformity with the analogy of faith. These same three periods are traceable in the doctrine of the infallibility of the Roman Pontiff. Down to the Council of Constance in the fifteenth century, the stability of the faith of Peter, and the immutability of the Roman Church or of the see of Peter, were the universal belief of the Church. This belief was not speculative only. It was exhibited in the public practice of the Church. Every public act of Rome was declared to rest on the stability of faith in the see of Peter, or of the Apostolic See, or of the successor of the apostle, or of the voice of Peter still teaching by his successor in his see. This *praxis* of the Church was immemorial, universal, and invariable in the declaration of faith and the condemnation of error. The amplest proof of this truth is to be seen in the relation of the Pontiffs to general councils, as in that of S. Leo to the Council of Chalcedon, which he guided in faith, confirmed, and in part annulled; in that of Celestine to the Council of Ephesus, which he also directed and confirmed; of Agatho to the third Council of Constantinople; and in the acts of S. Innocent the First and of S. Gelasius, upon whose authoritative acts alone the doctrine of original sin and the canon of Holy Scripture rested down to the Council of Trent. In those days the word "infallibility" had not been invented, but the thing existed in its most energetic reality. Perhaps, but for what is called the great Western schism, the word "infallibility" might never have been invented. It was an analytical expression to account for the stability of the Roman faith. In the midst of all contentions both sides believed that the Apostolic See could never be deceived by errors, nor deceive others by erring itself. Why? Because, they said, of the promise given to Peter. But during the time when two and three claimants to the See of Peter divided the nations of Europe, which was his successor? Then the distinction between the infallibility of the See of Peter and the fallibility of the person who sat in it was first introduced. This was the beginning of a second period, or the stage of analysis. Nobody so far departed from the tradition of faith as to deny the stability, solidity, immutability—which is equivalent to the infallibility—of the Apostolic See. They analysed this universal belief into two elements—the see and the person. They distinguished *inter sedem et in eâ sedentem*—" between the see and him that sat in it." Gerson and certain writers of the Old Sorbonne denied the infallibility of the person, while they affirmed the infallibility of the see. But another analysis was soon to be made into the two elements of the person and the primacy. It was soon perceived that the see is nothing in itself—that it derives all its authority from him who sits in it. The See of Peter is not the material chair, nor is it the collective body of the Church around it, but the successor of Peter, who bears the office of Peter, with the powers and promises attaching to it. Nevertheless, as in the example already given of the Immaculate Conception, centuries passed away while the Immaculate Nativity and the Immaculate Conception were still in discussion, so also centuries passed away while theologians discussed whether the stability or infallibility in faith attached to the person or to the office.

Gradually the opinion of the Old Sorbonne became nearly obsolete, and probably would have become extinct but for the conflict of Louis the Fourteenth against Innocent the Eleventh in the matter of the *Regale* or royal prerogative in ecclesiastical matters. It was this conflict that gave rise to the Four Articles of 1682 in which the denial of the infallibility of the head of the Church was first reduced to a public formula and propagated by royal and parliamentary edicts. It was no sooner published than it was on all sides condemned—by the University of Louvain, by the theologians of Liége, by the professors of Douai, by the Church in Spain, and by a plenary council in Hungary. Three weeks after the four articles appeared they were condemned by Innocent the Eleventh, afterwards by Alexander the Eighth, and a second time upon his death-bed. After the death of Alexander the Eighth, Louis the Fourteenth wrote to his successor, Innocent the Twelfth, to retract the acts of 1682; and the bishops who framed the acts wrote also to retract them. They were likewise again condemned by Pius the Sixth, and by the whole consensus of schools, theologians, and universities, except only the Sorbonne and those who were formed by it or adhered to it. It may be truly said that, under the weight of all these condemnations, the opinion which ascribed infallibility to the See of Peter, but denied it to his successor, like the opinion of the Immaculate Nativity, to continue the parallel, had gradually declined, and that the opinion which affirms the infallibility of the Pontiff had become certain; so that if an Œcumenical Council had been held at any time between 1682 and 1869, there can be no doubt that the infallibility of the head of the Church would have been defined. But the time of definition was not yet come. There existed still, not in the tradition of the Church nor in theology, but in the minds of some, an obscurity as to the distinction between the person and the office. Controversies still went on as to whether the infallibility be personal or official. By personal infallibility some thought that inspiration was attributed to the Pope to be used personally at his will. But the idea of a personal infallibility distinct from the office was never maintained by any theologian. This wild notion existed only in the minds of those who imputed it as an extravagance to their opponents. But they simply taught that the successor of Peter cannot err in faith. No Catholic theologian ever held more than this. The doctrine affirmed by the schools and by the Holy See was, that infallibility attaches to the office, and that the office is held not by many as if in commission, but by one. Infallibility is personal, therefore, only in the sense that the office is borne by a person. It was in this sense that the bishops in 1862 and in 1867 said that the voice of Pius was the voice of Peter. Peter's office, with all its prerogatives, is perpetual, and his office is borne by the person who succeeds to his place. But it is not necessary to dwell longer now upon this doctrine. We shall have time to do so when we come hereafter to the history of the definition.

9. Such, then, was the state of this question when the solemnities of the Centenary closed, and the bishops returned to their dioceses. Many at once published pastoral letters giving an account of the events in Rome. In some of these documents the intellectual and doctrinal significance of the Cen-

tenary was fully brought out.* For some years before, in France, Germany, and England, the force and value of the pontifical acts, and the obligation imposed by the doctrinal authority of the Pope in definitions of faith or in inflicting censures, had been in lively discussion, and it cannot be doubted that the Centenary had powerfully moved half the episcopate of the Church to desire that the Œcumenical Council should put an end to internal divergences on these points, so nearly affecting the doctrinal authority of the Holy See.

10. We have seen that on the 26th of June, 1867, Pius the Ninth announced to the Bishops his intention to convoke the Council. The date, however, was still undecided. This decision was made in the following year. In a Secret Consistory held on the 22nd of June, 1868, Pius the Ninth interrogated the cardinals whether they thought it expedient that the Œcumenical Council should be promulgated on the next feast of St. Peter and St. Paul, that is, the 29th of the same month, and its opening fixed for the 8th of December, 1869. The cardinals unanimously answered in the affirmative, and the Pope enjoined them to pray thenceforward for the especial assistance of the Holy Ghost.

* "The Centenary of S. Peter and the General Council." Longmans. 1867.

Inasmuch as the motives for which Pius the Ninth convoked the Council cannot be more directly known than from his own words and acts, it will be well to examine the text of the Bull of Indiction, which is dated the 29th of June, 1868. It runs as follows:—

Pius Bishop, servant of the servants of God, for perpetual remembrance. The only begotten Son of the Eternal Father, for the great love wherewith He loved us, that He might liberate mankind from the yoke of sin, the bondage of the devil, and the darkness of error, by which, through the sin of our first parents, it had been long and miserably oppressed, descended from the heavenly seat, but left not the glory of the Father, and, clothed in mortal array of the immaculate and most holy Virgin Mary, revealed the truth and way of life which He brought down from heaven, and having borne witness to it by many wonderful works, He delivered Himself for us as an Oblation and Sacrifice to God in the odour of sweetness.

After reciting the power given to the apostles to rule the Church which He had bought with His own blood, the Bull continues:—

And that the government of the Church should for ever proceed rightly and in order, and that the Christian people should ever abide in one faith, doctrine, charity, and communion, He promised both that He would be always present, even to the end of the world, and also from them all He chose Peter, and him He constituted to be the prince of the apostles, and His vicar here on earth, the head of the Church, its foundation and centre. . . . And forasmuch as the unity and integrity of the Church and the government of the same instituted by Christ needs to be stable and perpetual, therefore in the

Roman Pontiffs, the successors of Peter, who have been placed in this same Roman See, the same supreme power, jurisdiction, and primacy of Peter over all the Church abides in fulness of vigour.

The Bull then further says that

All men know with what unwearied care the Roman Pontiffs have laboured to guard the deposit of faith, the discipline of the clergy, the pure and learned education of the same, the holiness and dignity of matrimony, and day by day to promote more and more the Christian education of both sexes, to foster religion, piety, and integrity of morals among all people, to defend justice, and to provide also for the tranquillity, order, and prosperity of civil society.

Nor have they failed, when they judged it opportune, above all in times of grave perturbations and in the calamities of our most holy religion and of civil society, to convoke general councils, that with the councils and united strength of the bishops of the whole world, *whom the Holy Ghost has set to rule the Church of God*, they might with providence and wisdom dispose all things necessary for defining the dogmas of faith, for destroying the errors which prevail, for illustrating and developing doctrine, for upholding and restoring discipline, and for the correction of moral corruption among the peoples.

It is at this time evident and manifest to all men in how horrible a storm the Church is now tossed, and by what vast evils even the civil State is afflicted. For the Catholic Church, and its saving doctrine and venerable power, and the supreme authority of this Holy See, are by the bitterest enemies of God and man, assailed and trampled down; all sacred things are held in contempt, ecclesiastical possessions spoiled, and the ministers of holy things, men of conspicuous life dedicated to the divine service, and men of the highest Catholic excellence, harassed in every way; the religious orders suppressed, impious books of every kind, and pestilent documents, and manifold and most pernicious sects diffused on every side : the education of hapless youth, withdrawn everywhere from the clergy, and, what is worse, in not a few places intrusted to the teachers of iniquity and error.

Wherefore, following closely in the footsteps of our predecessors, we have judged it to be opportune to bring together into a General Council, which has long been our desire, all our venerable brethren, the ministers of the sanctuary, of the whole Catholic world, who have been called to share in a portion of our solicitude. . . . For in this Œcumenical Council must be examined with the greatest accuracy, and decreed, all things which, especially in these rough times, relate to the greater glory of God, the integrity of faith, the gravity of divine worship, the eternal salvation of men, the discipline of the secular and regular clergy, its wholesome and solid culture, the observance of ecclesiastical laws, the amendment of manners, and the instruction of Christian youth. . . . And with the most intent study care must be taken that all evils may be averted from the Church and from civil society. . . . For no man can deny that the power of the Catholic Church and of its doctrine bears not only upon the eternal salvation of men, but also promotes the temporal welfare of peoples, their true prosperity, order, and tranquillity, and also the progress and solidity of human sciences, as the annals of both sacred and profane history clearly and openly show by luminous facts, and demonstrate with constant evidence.

Having thus drawn in outline the work of the Council, and declared the motives of its convocation, Pius the Ninth solemnly convoked it in these words :—

Wherefore, resting upon and upheld by the authority of Almighty God, the Father, the Son, and the Holy Ghost, and of the blessed Apostles Peter and Paul, which we exercise on earth, by the counsel and assent of our venerable brethren the cardinals of the Holy Roman Church, we by these letters indict, announce, convoke, and ordain that the sacred Œcumenical and General Council be held in this our mother city of Rome in next year, 1869, to begin on the 8th day of December, sacred to the Immaculate Conception of the Virgin Mary, mother of God, and to be continued, and, by God's help, to be completed and ended for the glory of God and the salvation of all Christian people.

Then follows a paragraph of great moment :—

In this confidence we hope that God, in whose hands are the hearts of men, will, by his ineffable mercy and grace, bring it to pass that all sovereign princes and rulers of all peoples, above all such as are Catholic, seeing more clearly every day that the greatest benefits flow from the Catholic Church into the society of men, and that it is the firmest foundation of empires and kingdoms, will not only not hinder our venerable brethren from coming to the Council, but also earnestly favour and give them help, and studiously in all things, as becomes Catholic princes, co-operate with them in all things which may tend to the greater glory of God and the good of the Council.

> Given at Rome at S. Peter's in the year of our Lord's incarnation 1865, June 29. In the twenty-third of our Pontificate.

It seemed well to quote thus much from the text of the Bull of Indiction. If any man would ask why was the Council convened, here he has his answer. If any think that Pius the Ninth desired to be assured of his supreme power, he need only see with what apostolic boldness he asserts it here, and with what authority he wields it over the episcopate of the Universal Church.

We will now take up once more our narrative of events.

11. From the year 1833, when Gregory the Sixteenth condemned certain political writings in France, and from the year when Pius the Ninth condemned the attempt made in Germany by certain professors to withdraw politics and science from the cognisance and guidance of revelation, a school had existed in both countries hostile to the authority of Rome. It is therefore not to be wondered at that the acts and declarations of the Centenary should have called such adversaries into greater activity. In France appeared various writings of a lighter or of a more extensive kind, which need no longer be enumerated by name. In Germany, in the year 1868, appeared the work entitled *Janus*, an elaborate attempt of many hands to destroy, by profuse misrepresentations of history, the authority of the Pope, and to create animosity against the future Council. The fable, that the infallibility was to be defined by acclamation, was first formally announced in *Janus*. The work was promptly translated into English, French, and Italian. It was understood that in England and in France a number of writers had divided among themselves certain portions of historical controversy by which it was intended to render the definition of the infallibility impossible. An active cor-

respondence united ecclesiastical persons of several nations in co-operation for the same end. Conferences were held in France, Belgium, and Germany, to organise an opposition. Pamphlets and treatises were written on the eve of the assembling of the Council. But this was not all. In the year 1869, the Bavarian government was inspired to address itself to all the governments of Europe, inviting them to unite in opposition to the Council, which was to meet on the 8th of December in that year. A document was sent, dated the 9th of April 1869—that is, eight months before—with the signature of Prince Hohenlohe, then minister at Munich, the internal evidence of which revealed the hand from which it came. The object of these documents was to inspire all the civil powers of Europe with suspicion and alarm, and to combine them in active resistance to prevent the definition of the infallibility of the head of the Church. Prince Hohenlohe in his despatch said:—"The only dogmatic thesis which Rome would wish to have decided by the Council, and which the Jesuits in Italy and Germany are now agitating, is the question of the infallibility of the Pope." How Prince Hohenlohe should know the wish of Rome with such exclusive precision, he did not tell us. He then goes on to say:—"I thought the initiative in so important a matter should be taken by one of the great powers; but not having as yet received any communication on the subject, I have thought it necessary to seek for a mutual understanding which will protect our common interests," &c. A schedule of questions was then proposed to the theological faculty at Munich, intended to elicit answers for the purpose of obstructing the definition by alarming the powers of Europe. Answers were returned in the sense desired. But the questions and answers lost much of their effect because they were believed to come from the same hand. Nevertheless an extensive political and diplomatic party or conspiracy was formed, with the intention of hindering the expected definition. In the month of June following, Prince Hohenlohe addressed a second despatch to the governments of Europe. The Spanish minister, Olozaga, threatened the Church with the hostility of a league of France, Italy, Portugal, Spain, and Bavaria. An Italian minister addressed a circular to his diplomatic agents at the courts of Europe, inviting the powers to prevent the assembling of the Council. A joint despatch was sent by the Bavarian and Italian governments to the French government, urging the withdrawal of the French troops during the Council, *to insure the freedom of its deliberations*, or, in other words, to anticipate the 20th of September 1870 and the seizure of Rome.

An anonymous document was received by the bishops, which appeared simultaneously in French, English, German, Italian, and Spanish, elaborately arguing against the opportuneness of defining the infallibility of the Roman Pontiff. It was in certain countries distributed to the bishops by their governments. Such was the activity displayed in the ecclesiastical and diplomatic bodies. But there were other agencies at work. The newspapers of every country in Europe began to assail the future Council. Men of every sort of religion and of every shade of unbelief, by every kind of opposition from argument to derision, endeavoured to diminish beforehand the authority of the Council. It was said that it would not be œcumenical, because the Protestants would not sit in it; it would not be free, because the Pope would overbear the bishops. Then it was said that the bishops would not be able to discuss in Latin; that the Council would make new dogmas of matters not revealed; that no one would believe its definitions, or pay attention to its decrees. *Janus* had supplied all the adversaries of the Catholic faith and of the Catholic Church with a large vocabulary of vituperation, which was copiously directed against both.

12. The effect of this deliberate, wide-spread, and elaborate attempt to hinder the definition of the infallibility of the head of the Church, by

controlling the Council and obstructing its freedom, was as might be expected. It insured the proposing and passing of the definition. It was seen at once that not only the truth of a doctrine, but the independence of the Church, was at stake. If the Council should hesitate or give way before an opposition of newspapers and of governments, its office as Witness and Teacher of Revelation would be shaken throughout the world. The means taken to prevent the definition made the definition inevitable by proving its necessity. It was no longer a desire or conviction of individuals, but a sense of duty in the great majority of the bishops. But to this we shall have to return hereafter.

II. Having thus brought down the external events from the Centenary to the eve of the Council, we must take up again the narrative of the preparations that were making in Rome. We have seen that, by reason of the disturbed state of Europe and of Italy, the preparations were suspended in 1866. They were resumed on the 28th of July 1867, and were continued without interruption until they were completed just before the assembling of the Council.

1. The Commission of Direction consisted of five cardinal presidents, with eight bishops, and a secretary, the Archbishop of Sardis. Twenty-four Consultors were appointed for the Commission of

Dogma, nineteen for that of Discipline, twelve for the Commission on Religious orders, seventeen for the Commission of Foreign Missions and the East, and twenty-six for the Commission of Mixed or Politico-ecclesiastical Questions. The entire number of Consultors was one hundred and two, of which ten were bishops, sixty-nine secular priests, and twenty-three regulars: of these eight were Jesuits, four Dominicans, two Augustinians, one Barnabite, one Conventual Franciscan, one Minor Observant, one Benedictine, one Carmelite, one Servite, one minister of the Sick, and one Oratorian. Of these hundred and two thirty-one were from various nations invited to Rome.

The first question to be decided by the Commission of Direction was as to who had the right of sitting in the Council.

There could be no doubt as to the right of the episcopate at large; but a question arose as to bishops who had no ordinary jurisdiction such as vicars apostolic. There could, also, be no doubt as to their admissibility if invited, nor of their decisive vote when admitted. But the question was as to their right to be called. The decision arrived at was that it was fitting that they should be called to the Council according to the precedents and practice of the Holy See, and also lest their exclusion should give rise to questions as to the œcumenicity of the Council. The principle of this decision was that the Bulls by which councils have been convoked call together "archbishops, bishops, &c.;" therefore the axiom, "Ubi lex non distinguit, nec nos distinguere debemus," takes effect.

A letter of earnest and affectionate invitation was then written "to all bishops of the Churches of the Oriental Rite who are not in communion with the Apostolic See." This letter was presented to the patriarch of the Orthodox Greek Church, but he did not see fit so much as to open it. It was on that day, we are told, that four millions of Bulgarians notified to the same patriarch their withdrawal from his jurisdiction.

A letter was also written to all Protestants and other non-Catholics.

At the Council of Trent the same invitation was given, but with no happier result. Julius the Second published the condition on which they were invited— namely, a recognition of the divine authority of the Church. On no other condition could the Church invite them without abdicating its divine commission.

2. It will be hereafter seen of how great importance was also another question decided at this time by the Commission of Direction—that is, to whom it belongs to form the order or method by which the proceed-

ings of the Council should be regulated. After full discussion and a careful examination of the precedents of former councils, it was concluded that the forming of such order could ultimately belong to no authority except to the same which alone has the power to convene, to prorogue, to suspend, and to confirm the Council, or even to withhold confirmation from any or all of its acts. It was manifest that whensoever the head of the Church had invited the bishops in Council to express their pleasure as to the order to be observed, it had been done by way of prudence and from the desire to satisfy every reasonable wish. The experience of all numerous assemblies and even of General Councils shows that a supreme power of direction is often needed; and if this be true in assemblies of one nation, and with identity of habits and interests, how much more in an Œcumenical Council of many nations, among whom, being men, national sympathies and antipathies are often strong, notwithstanding their unity in faith. On the 29th of June 1869, it was therefore decided that the right of regulating the Council belonged to the authority which convened it, and that it was of the highest prudence to retain that right in the hands of him who is the head not only of the Council but of the Church. The importance of this, which may be called a vital law of the Church, will appear in our future narrative.

3. The chief points provided for in the order of proceedings were as follows:—

(1.) The proposition or introduction of matters to be treated.

(2.) The mode of discussion and of voting.

(3.) The attendance of the bishops.

(4.) The justification of absence.

(5.) The precedence in session.

(6.) The possible variances.

(7.) The mode of living.

(8.) The nature, number, and office of the officials of the Council.

(9.) The oath, or obligation of secrecy.

These points were defined after prolonged deliberation by the body of Consultors and published afterwards in the form of an Apostolical Constitution. All but the first two and the last points may be passed over in silence here; but on the right of proposition, the mode of discussion, and the secret, it may be well, in a narrative of the Vatican Council, to state briefly the course which was laid down.

We have already seen that there exists in the divine constitution of the Church no absolute necessity for the holding of councils—that the assembling of all bishops in one place is an usage of prudence, the expediency of which must be ultimately decided by the only authority which extends over all. No one but the head of the whole Church can lay on the bishops of the whole Church the duty of coming together. An archbishop may convene his province, and a patriarch his region of provinces, but no local authority can convene the universal episcopate. Therefore no one can constrain the head of the Church to convoke a council. It is an act of his own free will, guided by reasons of prudence, in order to obtain counsel upon the needs of the whole Church. He may, as we have seen that Pius the Ninth did, invite the fullest and widest counsel to ascertain beforehand what matters should be introduced or proposed for discussion ; and having done so, the self-evident dictates and the first instincts of prudence prescribe that the programme of subjects be fixed, precise, and limited. They can be limited by no authority except by that which is supreme.

But, inasmuch as in the course of discussion, and in the prolonged duration of a Council, it may be found that some subjects of moment have been passed over, or that new and important questions may emerge, provision was made for the introduction of new matter by the appointment of a special commission chosen by the Pontiff out of the members of the Council to assist him by their advice as to the introduction of any other propositions beyond those contained in the original programme. Every bishop was thereby able to lay

The True Story of the Vatican Council. 77

before this commission, in the form of a written petition to the Pontiff, any subject he might desire to see proposed to the Council. The Commission of Postulates, as it was called, after examination reported its judgment to the Pontiff, who gave orders as he might see fit. Anybody who will, with a just and sincere mind, weigh the reasonableness and the sufficiency of this provision cannot fail to acknowledge that without such a limit the discussions of an Œcumenical Council might be prolonged to any duration; any subject, howsoever needless and injurious, might be forced into discussion; the treatment of the most vital matters delayed, indefinitely obstructed, and even defeated altogether; the bishops detained for months or years from their dioceses, or the Council so thinned by their departure as to reduce it to a minority, and that, it may be, of the most pertinacious and the least pastoral bishops of the Church. Such, indeed, would be the way to expose the Council to the imputation of intrigues, cabals, and cliques. So much for its reasonableness. And as for its sufficiency, no petition which had in it reason enough to approve itself to a representative commission of five-and-twenty bishops chosen for their prudence and experience would be rejected; and certainly no petition which could not stand that ordeal ought to be proposed. The limitation of the right of proposition and the Commission of Postulates were the two securities of the Council itself against any unreasonableness or imprudence of its own members. The adversaries of the Vatican Council will not deny that, according to their estimate of its members, such securities were not needless; and the friends of the Council will acknowledge that in a body of 700 men there might well be found some for whom such temperate restraints were not unwise.

4. The other point of chief importance was the method of discussion. It would be unnecessary, and indeed impossible in the space of this short narrative, to give all the reasons which were alleged, and either accepted or laid aside by the Commission of Direction, as to the best mode of conducting the discussions. It may be truly said that this most critical and difficult question was treated with a minuteness and a fulness which left nothing unweighed. Passing over the reasons, we will explain the method.

It was decided that the preparatory labours of the 102 theologians and canonists should be digested into *schemata*, or draft decrees—that is into a definite and positive form giving the result of the patient labours of those who had been chosen out from many nations for their learning and experience.

These *schemata* were altogether the work of the bishops and theologians who prepared them. They had not so much as the shadow of the supreme authority upon them. The liberty of the Council to accept or to reject, to change or to modify them, was completely secured. The Pope, in his Constitution at the outset of the Council, told the bishops that the *schemata* had received no sanction from him, so that they might deal with them in all freedom.

The *schemata* were printed for the use of the Fathers of the Council. The method of examining them was as follows:—

(1.) The Council was to elect by secret vote within itself five commissions or deputations on: 1. Faith; 2. Discipline; 3. Missions; 4. Mixed Questions; 5. Rites.

(2.) The *schemata* were to be distributed to each of the members of the Council ten days at least before any discussion upon them would be opened.

(3.) The first discussion was in the general congregation of the whole Council. This first debate answered to the debate on the first and second reading of a bill in our legislature. If the bishops accepted the principle of the *schema*, they next proceeded to the second discussion on the details, or clauses as we should say, paragraph by paragraph, as in a committee of the whole house.

(4.) If objections were made, the whole discussion, taken in shorthand, was referred to the respective Commissions of Faith or Discipline, and the like, as the case might be.

(5.) The whole *schema* was then re-examined by the commission. It was amended, or even remodelled, and then reprinted and distributed again to the bishops, and submitted once more to a general congregation by a reporter deputed by the commission out of its own number.

(6.) After renewed discussion it was then put again to the vote, which might be given in three forms :— 1. *Placet*, or aye; 2. *Non Placet*, or no; 3. *Placet juxta modum*, or aye with modification, which is equivalent to voting for a bill on the second reading with the intention of amending it in committee. Those who voted *juxta modum* were required to send in their amendment in writing, which was printed, submitted to the deputation, and reported again to the general congregation for another voting.

(7.) If the *schema* so remodelled was further amended, the same process might be repeated. If, however, it was accepted by a majority of the Council, it was then passed by vote, and reserved for a final voting in the public session over which the Pope presided in person. The voting in Public Session, all discussion being over, was only by aye or no, by *placet* or *non placet*. This method of proceeding was published in the preliminary assembly of the Council by the Constitution *Multiplices inter* on the 6th of December, 1869. It underwent afterwards certain modifications by which the complete discussion of every subject was even more fully insured.

On this method we may observe that the liberty of speech was as perfectly secured as in our Parliament, and the accuracy of debate was even more completely provided for by the full and careful written amendments, and by the repeated remodelling of the *schema* by the commission or Select Committee before it returned to the Council—that is, to a committee of the whole house.

5. The only other point in the method for the regulation of the Council of which we need to speak is the obligation of secrecy. In the beginning of the Council of Trent this precaution was omitted; wherefore, on the 17th of February, 1562, the legates were compelled to impose the secret upon the bishops. If this was necessary in the sixteenth century, when the press had hardly come into existence, how much more so in the nineteenth, when whatever is said to-day is published over all the world to-morrow. It is obvious that for the treatment of such matters as were before the Vatican Council a complete independence and tranquillity of mind were necessary—a thing impossible under the relentless assaults of hostile governments and an ubiquitous press, with the perpetual harassing of half-informed friends and the incessant misrepresentations of enemies.

So much for the method and the regulations which were agreed to on the 3rd of November, 1869, by the commission of Direction, and confirmed by authority.

We now come to the last part of our narrative as to the events before the assembling of Council—namely, the matters to be discussed, of which it will be enough to give a list. They were six in number.

(1.) Schema on Catholic doctrine against the manifold errors flowing from Rationalism.

(2.) Schema on the Church of Christ.

(3.) Schema on the Office of Bishops.

(4.) Schema on the Vacancy of Sees.

(5.) Schema on the Life and Manners of the Clergy.

(6.) Schema on the Little Catechism.

On these, or at least on some of these, we shall have to speak hereafter. It will therefore be enough at this time to note one fact only.

6. In preparing the *schema* on the *Church of Christ*, which consisted of fifteen chapters, after a full treatment of the body of the Church the commission inevitably came to treat of its head. Two chapters were prepared: the one on the primacy of the Roman Pontiff, the other of his temporal power. In treating of the primacy it was likewise inevitable that the commission should come to treat of the endowments of the primacy, and, among these endowments, first of the divine assistance promised to Peter and in Peter

to his successors in matters of faith, or, in other words, of the infallibility. On the 14th and 21st of January, 1869, the commission treated of the nature of the primacy; on the 11th of February it reached the doctrine of infallibility. Two questions were then discussed: the one, 1. "Whether the infallibility of the Roman Pontiff *can* be defined as an article of faith;" the other, 2. "Whether it *ought* to be defined as an article of faith." To the first question the whole commission unanimously answered in the affirmative; to the second all, but one only, concurred in the judgment that the subject ought not to be proposed to the Council unless it were demanded by the bishops. The words of this judgment run as follows: *Sententia commissionis est, nonnisi ad postulationem episcoporum rei hujus propositionem ab Apostolica Sede faciendam esse.* ("The judgment of the commission is, that this subject ought not to be proposed by the Apostolic See except at the petition of the bishops.") The one dissentient Consultor was an inopportunist. The commission, therefore, never completed the chapter relating to the infallibility.

The Commission on Doctrine sat for twenty-seven months, and held fifty-six sessions, in which time it completed three, and only three, *schemata*. After the opening of the Council it met once only; and so its labours ended.

Two observations may be made on these facts. The first is that now, for a second time, when the subject of infallibility would, according to the adversaries of the Council, be expected to take the first place, it was deliberately set aside. The second observation is that Pius the Ninth had neither desire nor need to propose the defining of his infallibility. Like all his predecessors, he was conscious of the plenitude of his primacy. He had exercised it in the full assurance that the faith of Christendom responded to his unerring authority; he felt no need of any definition. It was not the head of the Church nor the Church at large that needed this definition. The bishops in 1854, 1862, 1867, had amply declared it. It was the small number of disputants who doubted, and the still smaller number who denied, that the head of the Church can neither err in faith and morals, nor lead into error the Church of which he is the supreme teacher, that needed an authoritative declaration of the truth.

As to the labours of the other sections, on Discipline, on Religious Orders, on Missions and the Oriental Churches, and on Rites, no comment need be made. The world has little interest in them, and takes no notice of them. The one object of its hostility is the Definition which has affirmed the divine authority of the head of the Church.

CHAPTER III.

THE OPENING OF THE COUNCIL: AND FIRST CONSTITUTION ON FAITH.

THE narrative of the Archbishop of Florence reaches to the date of the assembling of the Council. From this point we have, if possible, a still surer witness for the minute facts and dates which he has recorded. The Bishop of S. Pölten, in Austria, Monsignor Fessler, was appointed by Pius the Ninth to be Secretary to the Vatican Council. Through his hands every authoritative document passed; by him it was countersigned and distributed to the Council. He was necessarily present at every Public Session and every General Congregation. He was cognisant of the acts and decisions of the Cardinal Presidents. No one possessed such means of accurate and certain knowledge. There is a saying in S. Pölten that no bishop lives in that see longer than ten years. Monsignor Fessler was no exception. He took possession of his see in 1865, four years before the Council, and in four years after the Council he died. He has, however, left behind a small book which may be called a diary of the Council. He has there minutely registered the number of votings, and the number of votes by which each decree was passed. We have therefore a guidance in these points which cannot fail.

1. Early in December 1869, six days before the opening of the Council, a Preliminary Congregation was held in the Sistine Chapel in presence of Pius the Ninth. He expressed his joy at seeing so great a number of bishops gathered at his call from all parts of the world. He bade them, in entering the Council, to pray especially for charity, patience, and perseverance. After the allocution, the names of the Cardinal Presidents of the Council were announced, and those also of the other officials. The Constitution for the regulation of the Council was then distributed to the bishops.

On the 8th of December, the Feast of the Immaculate Conception, the first Public Session was held in the hall of the Council—that is, in the transept on the right hand of the Basilica of St Peter, or the Gospel side of the high altar, and close to the Confession of the Apostle.

After the *Veni Creator* had been sung, the Session opened with High Mass, at the end of which the Secretary of the Council placed upon the altar the Book of the Gospels, which always remained open throughout the Session. A sermon was then addressed to the Council, and the Synodal prayers were intoned by the Holy Father, followed by the Litany of the Saints. After the Gospel had been sung, the Pope made an allocution to this effect:—

> You are now met, venerable brethren, in the name of Jesus Christ, to bear witness with us to the Word of God; to declare with us to all men the truth, which is the way that leads to God; and to condemn with us, under the guidance of the Holy Ghost, the doctrines of false science. God is present in His holy place; He is with our deliberations and our efforts; He has chosen us to be His servants and fellow-workers in this great work of His salvation. Therefore, knowing well our own weakness, and filled with mistrust of ourselves, we lift up our eyes and our prayers to Thee, O Holy Ghost—to Thee, the source of true light and wisdom.

After the *Veni Creator* had been again sung, the Bishop of Fabriano from the *Ambo* read the decree of the opening of the Council, the substance of which was as follows:—

> Is it the pleasure of the fathers that the Œcumenical Council of the Vatican should be opened, and should be declared open for the glory of the most Holy Trinity, the custody and declaration of the faith and of the Catholic religion; for the condemnation of errors which are widely spreading, and for the moral correction of clergy and people?

The Council unanimously answered *Placet*. The Pope then declared the Council to be opened, and fixed the second Public Session for the Feast of the Epiphany, January 6, 1870. The Session closed with the *Te Deum* and the Pontifical benediction.

This detailed account is given because, with little variation, it describes all the Public Sessions which followed afterwards.

2. On the 10th of December the first General Congregation for business was held under the direction of the Cardinal Presidents. Cardinal de Luca held the first place in the stead of Cardinal de Reisach, who had before been named as the First President. He was at that time in Savoy in his last illness, which ended on Christmas-day. He was a man of great and varied learning, of a large and refined culture of mind, fitted in a special way to understand the diversities of thought which met in the Vatican Council. His loss to the Holy See, great as it would have been at any time, was still more seriously felt at the meeting of the Council, in preparing for which he had borne a chief part. Cardinal de Reisach was not only one of the foremost members of the Sacred College in the public service of the Church, but in private life he was greatly and deservedly loved for his genial and sympathetic character.

After the usual prayer at the commencement of the sitting, the list of names of the Commission of Postulates or Propositions, appointed by the Pope, was published. It was composed of cardinals who had had experience both as residents in Rome, and formerly as Nuncios in foreign courts, together with archbishops and bishops selected from each of the chief nations in the Council.

The list was as follows :—

Twelve cardinals—Patrizi, Antonelli, di Pietro, de Angelis, Barili, and Monaco; Cardinals Corsi, Archbishop of Pisa; Riario Sforza, Archbishop of Naples; Rauscher, Archbishop of Vienna; de Bonnechose, Archbishop of Rouen; Cullen, Archbishop of Dublin; Moreno, Archbishop of Valladolid.

Two patriarchs—Antioch and Jerusalem.

Ten Archbishops — Thessalonica, Sardis, Turin, Sorrento, Tours, Westminster, Valencia, Malines, Santiago in Chili, and Baltimore.

Two Bishops—Paderborn and Messina.

The other commissions were to be elected by the universal suffrage of the Council.

The commission of Faith, which consisted of twenty-five, was elected in the third General Congregation on the 20th of December, as follows :—The Archbishop of Edessa (Roman), Archbishop of Modena, the Bishop of Treviso and Calvi (Italian), the Archbishop Primate of Gran (Hungarian), the Bishop of Brixen (Austrian), the Bishops of Ratisbon and Paderborn (German), Archbishop of Cambrai and Bishop of Poitiers (French), Archbishop of Saragossa and Bishop of Jaen (Spanish), Archbishops of Westminster (English), of Cashel (Irish), of Utrecht

(Dutch), of Malines (Belgian), of Gnesen and Posen (Polish), the Bishop of Sion (Swiss), the Armenian Patriarch of Cilicia, and the Archbishop of Bostra (Asiatic), of Baltimore and San Francisco (North American), of Santiago in Chili, and Bishop of Rio Grande (South American). The Pope named Cardinal Bilio President of the Commission.

The Commission of Discipline was composed of twenty-four members, likewise selected from all nations — the Bishop of Birmingham representing England.

The Commission on Religious Orders was in like manner chosen — England being represented by the Bishop of Clifton.

The election of the other commissions was postponed.

3. The second Public Session was held on the Feast of the Epiphany. On that day was made the profession of faith by all members of the Council, according to the tradition of the Church. In the second Council of Constantinople, A.D. 381, the fathers repeated the Creed of the Council of Nicæa; at Chalcedon, A.D. 451, was recited the Creed of Nicæa, with the addition of the Council of Constantinople. So again in the subsequent Councils of Constantinople and the Second of Nicæa. In like manner also at Trent was recited the creed

of the former Councils; and in the Council of the Vatican the same was recited with the articles or definitions of the Council of Trent, which are called the Creed of Pius the Fourth.* First the Pope rose and recited the profession of faith in a loud voice. After that the Bishop of Fabriano read it from the *Ambo*. Then for two whole hours the cardinals, patriarchs, primates, archbishops, bishops, and other fathers of the Council made their adhesion to the same by kissing the Gospel at the throne of the head of the Church. Seven hundred bishops of the Church from all the world, the representatives of more than thirty nations and of two hundred millions of Christians, made profession with one heart of the same faith in the same form of words. If any one can believe this intellectual unity of faith, which has endured for eighteen hundred years unchanged through all changes, in all the minuteness of the definitions of Nicæa, Constantinople, and Trent, to be a simply human and natural fact, his credulity must be great. They who looked on, still more they who shared in that world-wide profession of the baptismal creed of the Christian world, will never forget it. Never at any time has such a witness been borne to the universality and unity of the Catholic faith.

* The Definitions of the Vatican Council are now in like manner added to those of the Council of Trent.

With this closed the second Public Session.

The first *schema*, or draft decree, 'On Catholic Faith, and on the errors springing from Rationalism,' containing eighteen chapters, was discussed by thirty-five bishops in the General Congregations between the 18th of December and the 10th of January. It was then sent back to the Commission on Faith to be entirely remodelled. The original *schema* was one of the grandest of theological documents, cast in the traditional form of conciliar decrees, taking its shape, as they did, from the errors which required condemnation. It was somewhat archaic perhaps in language, but worthy to rank with the decrees of the Councils of Toledo or of Lateran. It was referred to the Commission on Faith, and on the 14th of March it was again distributed to the Council in its new form, wholly recast, and was received with general approbation. The new document is of a distinct character, and ought not to be compared with its predecessor. Instead of eighteen chapters, it contained only an Introduction and four chapters, in which every sentence is full of condensed doctrine, and the whole has a singular beauty and splendour of divine truth impressed upon it. The commission was engaged on the task of recasting the *schema* until the end of February.

5. In order to show the sustained care and exact-

ness with which the work of the Council was conducted, and to remove from truthful and fair minds the notion that the Council cared little for anything but one subject, it will be well to give an account of the way in which this new *schema* was elaborated and finally adopted. A full statement will be given hereafter of the contents of this first *schema* on Catholic faith in the form in which it was finally passed. For the present it is enough to say that its subject-matter was what may be called the first foundations of natural and revealed religion—namely, the existence and perfections of God, the creation of the world, the powers and office of the human reason, revelation, faith, the relation of reason to faith, and of faith to science. From these truths followed the condemnations of atheism, materialism, pantheism, naturalism, and rationalism. To enter into these topics here would break the thread of this narrative. But they will be treated hereafter.

The second discussion began in the General Congregation on the 18th of March by a report made by the Primate of Hungary. Nine bishops then spoke in the general discussion of the text. No one desiring to speak further upon it, the general discussion closed, and the particular discussion of the first chapter began. In this debate sixteen took part; on the second chapter twenty; on the third twenty-two; on the fourth twelve spoke—in all seventy-nine. This discussion occupied nine sessions, and when no one desired to speak further, it closed. The *schema* was again sent back to the commission, with the amendments of the bishops. These were printed and distributed. After they had been examined by the commission a full report was made in the General Congregation on the Introduction, and the amendments were put to the vote. This being finished, the text of the Introduction was referred again. The four chapters were then each one treated in the same manner. On the first chapter there were forty-seven amendments. They were printed and distributed. The commission then reported, and the amendments were put to the vote. After another revision the first chapter was adopted almost unanimously on the 1st of April.

The second chapter had sixty-two amendments: the same process of reference to the commission, revision, reporting, and voting followed, and the chapter was referred back for final amendment.

The third chapter had one hundred and twenty-two amendments. These again were referred, printed, distributed, reported on, accepted or rejected, and the text once more returned to the commission. This took two days.

The fourth chapter had fifty amendments, which were treated as before, and sent back to the commission. This was on the 8th of April. On the same day the second chapter as amended was passed. The third and fourth were passed on the 12th of April— the one unanimously, the other all but unanimously. The whole was then put to the vote. There was no *Non placet*, but there were eighty-three *Placet juxta modum*. All these amendments were then sent in as before and printed in a quarto volume of fifty-one pages. On the 19th of April the report was made, and the amended text was unanimously accepted. In passing this one *schema* the interval between the 14th of March and the 19th of April was consumed; seventy-nine members of the Council spoke; three hundred and sixty-four amendments were made, examined, and voted upon; six reports were made by the commission upon the text, which, after its first recasting, had been six times amended.

The decree was finally adopted unanimously by six hundred and sixty-seven votes in the third Public Session, on the Dominica in Albis or Low Sunday, April 24, and confirmed by the Pope, who spoke as follows: "The decrees and canons contained in the Constitution just read were accepted by all the fathers, no one dissenting; and we, the Sacred Council, approving, by our apostolical authority so define and confirm them." He then went on to address the Council: "You see, beloved brethren, how good and pleasant it is to walk in the house of God in unity and peace. As our Lord gave to his apostles, so I, his unworthy Vicar, in his Name give peace to you. That peace, as you know, casts out fear; that peace shuts the ear to unwise words; that peace, may it go with you in all the days of your life; may that peace be with you in death; may that peace be your everlasting joy in heaven."

This account is given in full that a true estimate may be made of the care and deliberation with which the decrees of the Council were elaborated.

6. After the third Public Session followed the discussion on discipline relating to bishops, which lasted through seven sittings, in which thirty-seven spoke.

This again was followed by another relating to the clergy, which likewise occupied seven sittings and thirty-eight speakers.

Then followed the *schema* on the Little Catechism, which took up six sittings; forty-one speakers joined in it.

These discussions were not closed until no one desired to speak.

From these facts it will be evident that the amplest time and latitude of discussion was permitted from the outset of the Council, and the same will be hereafter still more manifest at its close.

All the *schemata* hitherto mentioned were referred

to the respective commissions for revision in accordance with the report of the speeches and the written amendments of the bishops.

The second *schema* on faith, relating to the Church, had been before distributed. It contained fifteen chapters and twenty-one canons. The first ten chapters related to the body of the Church; the eleventh and twelfth related to the primacy of the head of the Church; the last three treated of the relations of the Church to the civil powers. Ten days were given to study and to send in written observations on the *schema*. One hundred and twenty amendments in writing were sent in. Of these many were signed, not by the writer alone, but by a large number of names. For instance, one had twenty-nine signatures; a second, thirteen; a third, eleven; a fourth, eight; a fifth, seventeen; a sixth, ten; a seventh, twenty-four. Therefore these documents represented not less than two hundred members of the Council—that is, nearly a third of the whole number.

7. We have now come to a moment in the history of the Council to which we must devote a closer attention.

When it was found that the *Schema de Ecclesiâ* contained only two chapters on the head of the Church —that is, on the primacy and on the temporal power —a very large number of the bishops desired that the subject of the infallibility of the head of the Church should be added to complete the doctrine, which would otherwise remain in an unfinished state. We have already seen that the Commission of Direction, when it came to this point in preparing the *schemata*, suspended its work, and left the subject incomplete. The work, therefore, was to be begun over again, for no complete preparation existed.

The legitimate or constitutional course open to the bishops who desired that the doctrine of the infallibility should be introduced, was to present a petition to the Commission of Postulates or Propositions, asking that a chapter on the subject of infallibility should be added to the *schema*. It was necessary, therefore, to frame such a petition and to obtain the signatures of any members of the Council who desired the addition to be made.

While these things were being done, the bishops who thought the discussion of the infallibility would be, as they said, inopportune, were not inactive. About a hundred bishops signed a petition asking that the subject of the infallibility should not be laid before the Council.

And here it is a duty of justice to those who signed either of these two petitions that we should review the reasons for which some thought it inopportune that any such definition should be made, and others that it was not only opportune, but necessary.

8. A grave injustice has been done to the bishops who opposed the definition. The world outside the Church, not believing in infallibility, claimed them as its own. They were treated as if they denied the truth of the doctrine itself. Their opposition was not to the doctrine, but to the *defining* of it, and not even absolutely to the defining of it, but to the defining of it *at this time*. The chief and foremost of those who opposed the defining it in the Vatican Council had signed the Address of the Centenary, in which, as we have seen, were contained the acclamations of Chalcedon and of Constantinople. They were united in declaring that Peter spoke by Pius. How, then, could anyone so far wrong them as to say that they opposed the definition because they denied the doctrine to be true? They who were in the Council may be permitted to bear witness to what they heard and know. Not five bishops in the Council could be justly thought to have opposed the truth of the doctrine. This is the testimony of one who heard the whole discussion, and never heard an explicit denial of its truth. Arguments were indeed advanced which logically, if pushed to their conclusion, would seem to oppose the doctrine ; and representations of history were made which could not be

easily squared with the infallibility of the head of the Church. But these were heard in only two or three speeches made by bishops of the Council; and some of these had signed the Address of the Centenary, and one especially had taught the doctrine as a professor in a seminary.

But as the consistency of many has been involved in this question, it is right and just to treat it more fully.

Once for all let it be said in this place that the question whether the infallibility of the head of the Church be a true doctrine or not was never discussed in the Council nor even proposed to it. The only question was whether it was expedient, prudent, seasonable, and timely, regard being had to the condition of the world, of the nations of Europe, of the Christians in separation from the Church, to put this truth in the form of a definition. The infallibility of the Church had never been defined. Why then, it was asked, define it now? or, at least, why define the infallibility of its head?

Inasmuch as the arguments which were weighing in the minds of the bishops for and against the opportuneness of defining this doctrine were not—as controversialists, politicians, newspapers, and the religious adversaries of the Church would have men believe—arbitrary, factious, contentious, intriguing, servile, or unreasoning—it may be well to recite here in full a summary of the reasons on both sides. Those against the opportuneness come from a very high and authentic source, and were drawn up by one of the 102 theologians who prepared the *schemata* of the Council. He was one who held the doctrine as a divine truth in its amplest sense.

They shall be given here in full because they truly and adequately represent the balancing of motives which at that time caused some to hesitate, but decided the great majority.

9. The reasons against the definition were stated by a very learned and able theologian as follows :—

I. No necessity or urgent reason exists for such a definition, because the whole episcopate and the whole priesthood of the Church, and the whole body of the faithful, few excepted, have always received, and at this present time receive with veneration and docility, the doctrinal decisions of the Pontiffs, and recently those of Pius the Ninth.

II. For the determination of all controversies, and for the solution of all doubts, the decree of the Council of Florence respecting the supreme authority of the Roman Pontiff as universal doctor, together with the creed enjoined by Pius the Fourth after the Council of Trent, is sufficient.

III. In order to decide and to determine with exactness the question of the infallibility, it would not be enough simply to declare the Pope to be infallible. It would also be necessary to declare, and that by a decree, the form and the mode in which the infallibility of the Roman Pontiff is to be exercised and known ; which would be a difficult question, and would involve the authority of the Holy See in many new and grave complications.

IV. The making of such a definition would be exposed to

this grave difficulty. Suppose the bishops not to be unanimous, what course should then be taken? Suppose again that they were unanimous in declaring the infallibility of the Roman Pontiff to be a revealed doctrine, would they not, in the very act of defining the dogma, seem to profess that there is no authority in defining the faith inherent in the Episcopate?

V. Such a definition would not only be of doubtful utility. It would probably hinder the hope of reuniting the Eastern Churches to the Holy See, for the Greeks and Orientals recoil from every new word. It is well known what serious and endless controversies the single phrase " Filioque " has stirred up. For which reason, in the profession of faith enjoined by Gregory the Thirteenth for the Greeks, and by Urban the Eighth and Benedict the Fourteenth for the other Orientals, the very words of the Florentine decree, without any change or addition, were retained.

VI. Such a definition might retard also the return, which we so much desire, of Protestants to the unity of the Church, inasmuch as the new dogma would excite and increase in large numbers a prejudice against the Catholic Church, and especially against the Roman Pontiff, thereby rendering it more difficult for them to understand and to embrace the faith by raising a suspicion that the doctrine of the Pope's infallibility is a novelty unknown in earlier ages.

VII. This question might possibly raise divergencies among the bishops, who now are of one mind and heart in their reverence and obedience to the Holy See; a result which would be most disastrous.

VIII. The defining of the Pope's infallibility might also cause doubts, or, what is worse, dissensions among Catholics who are otherwise sound, and willingly submissive, from conviction, to the authority of the Church; and that because certain historical facts and documents are not as yet sufficiently explained, so that in many countries the minds of men are not yet prepared for such a definition.

IX. Such a new decree would be no remedy for the perversity of the few persons who reject the decisions of the Supreme

Pontiff and appeal from them to a General Council, as to a higher judge of controversies, forasmuch as their error comes not from the intellect, but from perversity of will. There is a difference, also, between a definition of the infallibility of the Pope and that of any other Christian doctrine. In the latter case, the authority of the Church may be sufficient to overcome any doubt. In the former it is the authority itself, the principle of all certainty in faith, which is in question. Would it not, therefore, be more prudent to spare the weakness of those who are not yet able to bear this definition?

X. It may be feared also, lest, by a perversion of the true sense of such a decree, some may be induced to despise the authority given by our Lord to bishops, especially in the condemnation of rash and pernicious opinions in philosophy and theology.

XI. Again it may be feared lest bishops, whom for some years the Holy See has been calling into activity, by discouraging them from sending to Rome in the first instance all doubts about books and matters of which it is their office to judge, might by such a definition be rendered more slack and backward in exercising their episcopal office of judges of doctrine.

XII. It soon, probably, would follow from such a definition, by reason of the nature of man, that not only matter of doctrine on which the supreme decision of the Church is desired, but other kinds of business also, would be sent to Rome for decision, so that everything would crowd in upon the centre of unity. And great as are the experience, prudence, and authority of the Roman congregations, such a course would not be for the prosperity of the Universal Church; for the Church, as the Holy Ghost teaches, is a body, but the health of a body depends on the force and motion of all and each of the members. "If all were one member, where were the body?" (1 Cor. xii. 19). Nobody doubts that the chief member of the body is the head, and that in it, as in its centre and seat, the vital force and guidance reside; and yet no one will say that the soul resides in the head alone, which is rather diffused as its form throughout the members of the whole body.

These, then, were some of the reasons for believing that a definition of the infallibility of the Pope would not be opportune. They who held these opinions said:

Let that suffice which has been already declared and has been believed by all—namely, that the Church, whether congregated in Council or dispersed throughout the world, is always infallible, and the Supreme Pontiff, according to the words of the Council of Florence, is "the teacher of the whole Church and of all Christians." But as to the mysterious gift of infallibility, which by God is bestowed upon the Episcopate united to the Pope, and at the same time is bestowed in a special manner on the Supreme Pontiff, it may be left as it is. The Church, as all Catholics believe, whether in an Œcumenical Council, or, by the Pope alone, without a Council, guards and explains the truths of revelation. It is not expedient or opportune to make further declarations unless a proved necessity demand it, which necessity at present does not appear to exist.

10. On the other hand, it was urged by those to whom these reasons appeared to be insufficient:

I. That if the Episcopate, priesthood, and people are, with so few exceptions, unanimous in receiving with submission and assent the Pontifical acts, there would not only be no risk in promulgating such a definition, but they would rejoice to see their submission justified by an authoritative definition; or, if the number of those who refuse submission be greater, a necessity would thereby be proved for the declaration of the truth.

II. That the decree of the Council of Florence ought indeed to be sufficient, and would be so if it were not misinterpreted by those who deny the infallibility of the Supreme Pontiff speaking *ex cathedra*. The existence of this misinterpretation by Gallicans and by Anglicans shows that the decree is not sufficient.

III. That the doctrine of the infallibility of the Pope, held, as it is alleged, by all but a small number, may indeed be exposed now to the questions as to the form and mode of its exercise. These questions will not become less clear by being defined, that is, by being made more clear. The complications which now arise from want of a clear declaration would then be avoided. Erroneous or doubtful opinions give rise to complications; but truth excludes doubt and obscurity in proportion as it is precisely defined.

IV. That if the bishops were not unanimous as to the making of a definition, no doubt the Council would know in its prudence what course to take. The Council of Trent made no definition of the Immaculate Conception. It went to the very verge of defining it, but no further. If the bishops were unanimous in declaring the prerogatives of the head of the Church, they would not thereby abdicate or divest themselves of any privileges or endowments divinely conferred upon the Episcopate. The divine endowments of the Church are not at war with each other. The apostles did not cease to be infallible because their Head was so. The infallibility of the Church does not diminish the infallibility of Councils. The endowments of the body are the prerogatives of the head. Both have their proper sphere and their full and legitimate exercise. No bishop alone is infallible, nor is the whole Episcopate infallible without its head. Of what, then, could they divest themselves by declaring their head to be infallible?

V. That all hope of reunion with the East is alone to be found in an explicit recognition of the divine prerogatives of the Church. Reunion on anything short of this, on any principle, obscure, ambiguous, or equivocal, could not endure for a day. The rent would be made worse. The decree of the Council of Florence, which is alleged to be sufficient, was not sufficient for the Greeks. They accepted it for a moment, but no sooner were they again at Constantinople than they threw it to the winds. Reunion is not to be gained or to be sought by reducing its conditions, like a bargain, to the minimum, but by an explicit and precise acceptance of the truth. Gregory the Thirteenth, Urban the Eighth, Benedict the Fourteenth, kept strictly to the

Florentine decree, because no other existed then. No other exists at this day; and the question is, whether the events of the last three centuries do not demand a more precise declaration of the truth.

VI. That the return of Protestants also to the Church is more retarded now by the apparent contradiction among Catholics on the subject of infallibility, than it could be by the definition of the infallibility of the Pope. They now reject the infallibility of the Church altogether, because they believe that we are divided, if not about the infallibility of the Church, at least about the infallibility of its head. So long as the infallibility of the Pope is not authoritatively declared, they cover themselves under the shelter of those Catholics who deny it. And, to our shame, they borrow their belief that the opinion is a novelty from some among us. The Gallicans put weapons into their hands which they use against all infallibility whatsoever.

VII. That no divergence among the bishops is to be feared, the unanimity alleged above may assure us. But if it were to exist, would it be of greater moment than the want of unanimity on the doctrine of the Immaculate Conception at the Council of Trent? The prudence of the Council, both natural and supernatural, would know how to deal with such a contingency; and if divergence in anything should arise, no diminution of filial and cordial obedience to the Holy See could follow in those things where all are unanimous.

VIII. That, if the pastors of the Church be unanimous, there is no fear of dissensions or doubts among the faithful. Rather, the dissensions and doubts, if any now exist, arise from the allegation that the pastors are not unanimous as to the infallibility of the Vicar of Jesus Christ. It is of the highest moment to put an end to this false allegation, so boldly and plausibly made by non-Catholics of every name. For this reason alone the sooner the unanimity of the pastors of the Church can be manifested the better, both for the truth's sake and for the salvation of souls. The same reason holds as to the supposed historical difficulties. They have been examined and exposed over and over again; but they will be perpetually brought up again, and with increased confidence, so long as the infallibility of the Roman Pontiff shall be left undefined. Where the Church has spoken, the faithful are not open to seduction. While the Church is silent, the spirits of error are clamorous and plausible. A definition would silence all voices, the voice of the Church alone excepted.

IX. That any decree would satisfy those who, out of perversity, oppose the faith, by appealing from the Supreme Pontiff to a General Council, and excommunicate themselves, is not to be expected. But if there be a hope for them, it is to be found in rendering clear beyond all possibility of doubt the divine certainty of faith. But this is closely connected with the divine authority of the head of the Church. The example of our Lord in sparing the infirmities of the weak, who were as yet unable to bear mysteries not yet revealed, is no warrant for keeping back any revealed truth because men will not believe the revelation already made. This would tacitly assume that the infallibility of the head of the Church is not a revealed truth. If it be a revealed truth, our Lord's example is not in point; still less that of the apostles, who "kept back nothing," and declared to the faithful " all the counsel of God " (Acts xx. 20, 27).

X. That the perverse interpretation of a decree could only be partial, and could never be either widespread or permanent. Such perversion, therefore, can be no reason against the definition being made, if the proper reasons exist for making it. The definition of the infallibility of the Roman Pontiff can in no way lessen the authority of bishops as judges of doctrine in their own flocks, but on the contrary it would give great support to all their legitimate acts. It does not appear how bishops should be more authoritative because their head is believed to be less so.

XI. That, for the same reason, it does not appear probable that bishops would be less active as pastors and judges in their own Churches because the doctrine which they already unanimously believe had been declared by a final definition. If the belief of its truth does not now produce these consequences, it does not yet appear why the defining of that truth should do so.

XII. That, lastly, no centralisation of the ordinary and diocesan administration of the Universal Church could be in any way promoted by a definition of the infallibility of the Vicar of Jesus Christ, speaking *ex cathedrâ*, in matters of faith and morals. Such a definition belongs to a higher order, with which the ordinary pastoral office of bishops can rarely have any contact. Questions of faith and morals, on which the Church has not already judged, very seldom arise in any diocese. The infallibility here in question has no relation to the multifarious administration of dioceses. Such a definition would either have no appreciable influence on the ordinary administration of bishops, or, if any, only in the way of giving greater certainty to their judicial acts, and to the pastoral jurisdiction of the Episcopate throughout the world.

For these reasons it appeared to others that the objections to such a definition had no sufficient weight to dissuade the Council from making it.

11. But thus far we have only answered objections. It now may be well to state the positive reasons which decided the majority of the bishops to sign the petition by which they asked for the introduction of the subject of the infallibility, and in the end to define it.

I. They thought that such a definition would be opportune because the doctrine is true; for if true, how can it be said that to declare it is not opportune? Is not this question already closed by the fact that God has thought it opportune to reveal it? Can it be permitted us to think that what He has thought it opportune to reveal, it is not opportune for us to declare? It is true indeed that, in revealing the faith, God in his wisdom was slow, deliberate, and gradual, measuring his light to the infirmities of the human intelligence, and preparing the minds of men for a fuller manifestation both of his presence and of his kingdom. But this divine procedure, binding as it might be on us in dealing with heathen nations who have never heard his name, can be no rule for us, nor even lawful for us, in dealing with those who have been baptised into the full light of faith. From them nothing may be kept back. With them no economy can be admitted. There is now no "disciplina arcani" among the members of his mystical body. "That which you hear in the ear, preach ye on the house tops" (S. Matthew x. 27).

By "opportune," then, in the mind of the objector, must be meant something politic or diplomatic, some calculations of local expediency in respect to nations and governments. This sense of opportunity is proper to legislatures and cabinets in deliberating on public utilities and opinions; but in the Church, and in the truths of revelation, it is always opportune to declare what God has willed that men should know. If the infallibility of the head of the Church be a doctrine of revelation, then "necessity is laid upon us, and woe unto us if we preach not the Gospel" (1 Cor. ix. 16). It may, however, be said that many revealed truths are not defined; and that it does not follow that any doctrine ought to be defined, only because it is true, or because it has been revealed.

II. This is indeed certainly true, and would be of weight if this revealed truth had never been denied. There are two reasons for which the Church from the beginning has defined the doctrines of faith: the one to make them clear, definite and precise; the other to defend them and to put them beyond doubt when they have been called in question. If the infallibility of the head of the visible Church had never been denied, it might not have been necessary to define it now. The true doctrine of justification was never defined till it was denied. The nature of inspiration has never yet been defined, but the denial which is now spreading may one day make it necessary to define it. In like manner the infallibility of the Roman Pontiff has been openly denied. Its definition, therefore, has become necessary. It was never indeed formally denied before the period of the

Council of Constance; but this denial of the truth, modern as it is, renders its definition necessary. When this is said, objectors tell us that the denial is far more ancient and widespread. If that were true, it only makes the definition all the more necessary. They who, to make the doctrine appear doubtful, or to prove it to be false, represent the denial of it to be ancient and widespread, in that proportion increase the necessity of declaring it by an authoritative decree. Such a denial as emanated from the Assembly in 1682 would amply suffice to show that the definition would be more than opportune.

III. And further, the denial of the infallibility of the head of the Church has already suggested doubts as to the truth of the doctrine in minds that never doubted before. We are asked by non-Catholics, " If the doctrine be revealed, how is it that you allow it to be denied? If you are not doubtful about it, why not put it beyond doubt by declaring it to be true?" It is certain that not only Protestants believe the doctrine to be an open question among Catholics, but even among Catholics some are tempted to believe it to be doubtful, and therefore not revealed. They hear it said that it is irreconcileable with history, a modern exaggeration arising from the adulation of courtiers and the ambition of Popes. In France, to deny it has been thought a test of political independence. In England some Catholics are frightened by the pretensions of patristic learning and historical criticism of anonymous writers, so as to doubt or to shrink in false shame from believing a truth for which their fathers died. The admission of a doubt as to any revealed doctrine is fatal to faith in that doctrine.

IV. It would appear not only to be opportune that this doctrine should be placed beyond the reach of doubt by a definition, but that such a definition would be specially opportune at this time, because of the fact that the formal and systematic denial of the truth in question has arisen since the last General Council.

It may at first sight appear that this statement is at variance with the common assertion that the denial of the infallibility of the Roman Pontiff had its rise in the period and events of the

Council of Constance. It is true that an erroneous opinion lingered on from the time of the Council of Constance, in what De Marca calls the "Old Sorbonne," to distinguish it from the Sorbonne of his own day. But it is certain, then, that before the Council of Trent this opinion had not assumed the definite and elaborate form given to it by the Assembly of 1682, and by those who for two centuries have defended the Four Articles. This modern and dogmatic form of the denial of the Pope's infallibility, *ex cathedrâ*, was completed in the seventeenth century—that is, since the last General Council—and gave rise to a widespread and mischievous controversy.

V. It was therefore evident that if an Œcumenical Council should meet and separate without taking notice of this denial, one of two inferences would be drawn. It would be said either that Gallicanism had obtained its place among tolerated opinions ; or, at least, that it might be held with impunity. It does not readily appear what answers could be made to this argument. It would be hardly enough to say that it was not thought opportune to meet so open a denial of a doctrine universally believed and taught everywhere out of France, or that it was inopportune to renew the acts of three Pontiffs who had authoritatively censured it. History would have said of the Vatican Council : " Qui tacet, consentire videtur."

VI. It could not be said that the denial of the infallibility of the Roman Pontiff is an obscure and inert error. It is notorious and active. To find or invent a division among Catholics is the chief hope of antagonists. To foment the least divergence among Catholics into a conflict is their chief policy. There can be no doubt that this controversy afforded them their most advantageous attack. Catholics are visibly united on all doctrines of faith, but on the infallibility of the head, as distinct from the infallibility of the Church, a divergence existed which adversaries think or pretend to be a contradiction in faith. The combined action of a certain school within the Church, and of Protestants without it, has given to this erroneous opinion a great notoriety in the last two centuries, and this takes it out of the category of innocuous errors which may be left to evaporate or to die out of themselves. It had forced itself into the history of the Church, and would live on until, by the Church, it should be finally condemned.

VII. Prudence would require the condemnation of any notorious error which, even if innocuous at first, might hereafter produce ill effects ; but the denial of infallibility in the head of the Church had already produced ill effects. Nevertheless, so long as no final condemnation was stamped upon the error, it would always pass for a tolerated opinion. Men will never believe that it is wrong to do that which they see done with impunity every day. Where there is no law there is no transgression.

VIII. But the true and ultimate reason which determined the majority of the bishops to define the infallibility of the head of the Church was to protect from denial or doubt the divine certainty on which the revelation of Christianity comes down to us. We believe in revelation because God is its author. We know what he has revealed because the Church by divine assistance guards it. He might have ordained other ways for the custody and declaration of His truth. But the way he has actually ordained is a visible body of witnesses in perpetual succession with a special assistance of His presence and guidance. All Catholics believe that the Church, by the assistance of the Holy Ghost, is infallible, and therefore that all doctrines proposed by it for our belief are divine, and for that reason certainly true. But if the head of the Church may err in his teaching, doctrines may be proposed by him that may not be divine, and would therefore be doubtful. But if the teaching of the head of the Church cannot exclude doubt, for that reason it cannot form a foundation of faith. Where faith is, doubt cannot be ; and where doubt is faith ceases to be. If therefore it be left in doubt whether the teaching of the head of the Church be certainly true, those who believe that he may err can always contradict his teaching. A fallible head to an infallible body is a doctrine which would soon give way before the logic of common sense, and the denial of the infallibility of the head of the Christian Church is the first position of vantage to assail the infallibility of the Church as a whole, and therefore to assail the divine certainty of Christianity altogether.

IX. The infallibility of the Church dispersed or congregated in Council is matter of necessary faith. The infallibility of the eighteen General Councils in which the Church has been congregated is also of necessary faith. But the Church, during the last eighteen centuries, has done many acts of supreme importance by its head alone. Are these acts fallible or infallible? For instance, the declaration of original sin by Innocent the First, and of the canon of Holy Scripture by Pope Gelasius—are these declarations in matter of faith fallible or infallible? Are they doubtful or indubitable? The question has been formally raised, and must, for the sake of divine truth, be as formally solved. Surely this question, at least, cannot be left in doubt. The Church must decide what its members are to believe, or its office as a teacher is at an end.

12. Such were the reasons which finally determined 450 fathers of the Council to send up to the Commission of Postulates a petition that the doctrine of the infallibility of the head of the Church should be discussed in the Council.

The steps taken to prepare and to obtain signatures to this petition were as follows:—

A number of bishops of all nations met to agree upon the wording of the petition. After one or two revisions it was finally adopted in these words:

> The undersigned fathers humbly and earnestly beg the holy Œcumenical Council of the Vatican to define clearly, and in words that cannot be mistaken, that the authority of the Roman Pontiff is supreme, and therefore exempt from error, when, in matters of faith and morals, he declares and defines what is to be believed and held, and what is to be rejected and condemned, by all the faithful.

H

This was then printed for distribution.

It was decided that this petition should be sent with a circular letter to all the bishops, omitting only those whose known opposition made it a duty of delicacy and of respect not even to seem to obtrude upon them. It was afterwards decided to add to this brief petition, in an appendix, a series of reasons and of authorities from Provincial Councils in support of the petition. The whole was therefore printed a second time. And this perhaps has given rise to the mistake that there were two such petitions, of which the first failed, the second succeeded. There never was but one—the general petition here given—twice printed, indeed, but one and the same from first to last.

The whole of this action, which has been represented as conspiracy, cabal, intrigue, done in the dark, with suddenness and surprise, was done in open day. The petition was at once printed and given to all who wished for it. No sooner was it in print than an archbishop known to be of the opposition came and asked for a copy. He at once received three, and by the end of the week the petition came back to Rome in the *Augsburg Gazette* translated into German. It appeared at once in the journals of France, Switzerland, Italy, and England. So much for its clandestinity. Its authors wished it to be spread far and wide, and were thankful not only to friends but to adversaries who helped to make it more extensively known.

13. The text of the reasons and appendix added to the petition was as follows:—

REASONS FOR WHICH THIS DEFINITION IS THOUGHT OPPORTUNE AND NECESSARY.

The Sacred Scriptures plainly teach the primacy of jurisdiction of the Roman Pontiff, the successor of St Peter, over the whole Church of Christ, and, therefore, also his primacy of supreme teaching authority.

The universal and constant tradition of the Church, as seen both in facts and in the teaching of the fathers, as well as in the manner of acting and speaking adopted by many Councils, some of which were Œcumenical, teaches us that the judgments of the Roman Pontiff in matters of faith and morals are irreformable.

In the Second Council of Lyons, with the consent of both Greeks and Latins, a profession of faith was agreed upon, which declares: "When controversies in matters of faith arise, they must be settled by the decision of the Roman Pontiff." Moreover, in the Œcumenical Synod of Florence, it was defined that "the Roman Pontiff is Christ's true Vicar, the head of the whole Church, and father and teacher of all Christians; and that to him, in blessed Peter, was given by Jesus Christ the plenitude of power to rule and govern the Universal Church." Sound reason, too, teaches us that no one can remain in communion of faith with the Catholic Church who is not of one mind with its head, since the Church cannot be separated from its head even in thought.

Yet some have been found, and are even now to be found, who, boasting of the name of Catholic, and using that name to the ruin of those weak in faith, are bold enough to teach that sufficient submission is yielded to the authority of the Roman

Pontiff, if we receive his decrees in matters of faith and morals with an obsequious silence, as it is termed, without yielding internal assent, or, at most, with a provisional assent, until the approval or disapproval of the Church has been made known. Anyone can see that by this perverse doctrine the authority of the Roman Pontiff is overturned, all unity of faith dissolved, a wide field open to errors, and time afforded for spreading them far and wide.

Wherefore the bishops, the guardians and protectors of Catholic truth, have endeavoured, especially now-a-days, to defend in their synodal decrees, and by their united testimony, the supreme authority of the Apostolic See.

But the more clearly Catholic truth has been declared, the more vehemently has it been attacked both in books and in newspapers, for the purpose of exciting Catholics against sound doctrine, and preventing the Council of the Vatican from defining it.

Though, then, hitherto many might have doubted the opportuneness of declaring this doctrine in the present Œcumenical Council, it would seem now to be absolutely necessary to define it. For Catholic doctrine is now once more assailed by those same arguments which men, condemned by their own conscience, used against it in old times; arguments which, if carried to their ultimate consequences, would bring to the ground the very primacy of the Roman Pontiff and the infallibility of the Church itself; and to which, also, is frequently added the most violent abuse of the Apostolic See. Nay, more; the most bitter assailants of Catholic doctrine, though calling themselves Catholics, are not ashamed to assert that the Synod of Florence, which so clearly declares the supreme authority of the Roman Pontiff, was not Œcumenical.

If then the Council of the Vatican, being thus challenged, were to be silent, and omit to give testimony to the Catholic doctrine on this point, then Catholics would, in fact, begin to doubt the true doctrine, and the lovers of novelty would triumphantly assert that the Council had been silenced by the arguments brought forward by them. They would, moreover, abuse this silence on every occasion, and openly deny the obedience due to the judgments and decrees of the Apostolic See in matters of faith and morals, under pretext that the judgment of the Roman Pontiff is fallible on such points.

Wherefore the public good of Christianity seems to require that the holy Council of the Vatican, professing once again, and explaining more fully, the Florentine decree, should define clearly, and in words that can admit of no doubt, that the authority of the Roman Pontiff is supreme, and therefore exempt from error, when in matters of faith and morals he decrees and ordains what is to be believed and held by all the faithful of Christ, and what to be rejected and condemned by them.

There are, indeed, some who think that this Catholic truth should not be defined, lest schismatics and heretics should be repelled yet further from the Church. But, above all other considerations, Catholics have a right to be taught by the Œcumenical Council what they are to believe in so weighty a matter, and one which has been of late so iniquitously attacked, lest this pernicious error should in the end infect simple minds and the masses of people unawares. Hence it was that the fathers of Lyons and of Trent deemed themselves bound to establish the doctrine of the truth, notwithstanding the offence that might be taken by schismatics and heretics. For if these seek the truth in sincerity, they will not be repelled, but, on the contrary, drawn towards us, when they see on what foundations the unity and strength of the Catholic Church chiefly repose. But should any leave the Church in consequence of the true doctrine being defined by the Œcumenical Council, these will be few in number, and such as have already suffered shipwreck in the faith; such as are only seeking a pretext to abandon that Church by an overt act, which they plainly show they have deserted already in heart. These are they who have never shrunk from disturbing our Catholic people; and from the snares of such men the Council of the Vatican ought to protect the faithful children of the Church. For all true Catholics, taught and accustomed to render the fullest obedience both of thought and word to the Apostolic decrees of the Roman Pontiff, will receive with joyful and devoted hearts the definition of the Council of the Vatican concerning his supreme and infallible authority.

APPENDIX.

DECISIONS OF PROVINCIAL SYNODS RECENTLY HELD, SHOWING THE COMMON OPINION OF BISHOPS CONCERNING THE SUPREME AND INFALLIBLE AUTHORITY OF THE ROMAN PONTIFF IN MATTERS OF FAITH AND MORALS.

1. The Provincial Council held at Cologne in 1860, to which, in addition to his Eminence Cardinal Geissel, Archbishop of Cologne, five bishops subscribed, expressly declares: 'He (the Roman Pontiff) is the father and teacher of all Christians, *whose judgment in questions of faith is "per se" unalterable.*'

2. The bishops assembled in the Provincial Council, held at Utrecht in 1865, most openly assert: 'We unhesitatingly hold that the judgment of the Roman Pontiff in matters which refer to faith and morals is *infallible*.'

3. The Provincial Council of Prague in 1860, to which his Eminence Cardinal Archbishop Frederic de Schwarzenberg and four other bishops subscribed, under the heading, 'On the Primacy of the Roman Pontiff,' decreed as follows: 'We reject, moreover, the error of those who pretend that the Church can exist anywhere without being joined in bonds of union with the Church of Rome, in which the tradition which has been handed down by the apostles has been preserved by those who are in every part.'*

'We know that no one who is not joined to the head can be considered as a member of the body of the Church which Christ founded on Peter, and established on His authority. Let all them prefer to confess with us and with the multitude of orthodox believers spread over the whole world, the headship

---

* S. Irenæus, Adv. Her. 1. 3, c. 3, n. 2.

of the Roman Church and the primacy of the Roman Pontiff; let them, as is fitting, with us, reverence and honour with dutiful affection our Most Holy Father, Pius the Ninth, by God's Providence Pope, the lawful successor of the Prince of the Apostles, the Vicar of Christ on earth, the chief teacher of faith, and pilot of the ship of Christ, to whom *the most exact obedience and internal assent is due from all who wish to belong to the fold of Christ.* We declare and teach, that this authority of the Roman Pontiff comes from Christ our Lord, and that consequently it is dependent upon no power or favour of men, and remains unimpaired in all times, even in the most bitter persecutions which the Church of Rome has suffered, as was the case during the imprisonment and martyrdom of blessed Peter.'

4. The Provincial Council of Kalocza, held in 1860, declared: 'That as Peter was . . . the irrefutable teacher of the doctrines of faith, for whom the Lord Himself prayed that his faith might not fail, so his legitimate successors seated aloft on the Chair of Rome . . . preserve the deposit of faith with supreme and irrefutable powers of declaring the truth. . . . Wherefore we also reject, proscribe, and forbid all the faithful of this province to read or maintain, and much more to teach, the propositions published by the Gallican clergy, in 1682, which have already been censured this same year by the Archbishop of Gran, of pious memory, and by the other bishops of Hungary.

5. The Plenary Council of Baltimore, which met in 1866, and to which 44 archbishops and bishops subscribed, says: 'The living and infallible authority flourishes in that Church alone which was built by Christ upon Peter, who is the head, leader, and pastor of the whole Church, whose faith Christ promised should never fail; which ever had legitimate Pontiffs, dating their origin in unbroken line from Peter himself, being seated in his Chair, and being the inheritors and defenders of the like doctrine, dignity, office, and power. And because, where Peter is, there also is the Church, and because Peter speaks in the person of the Roman Pontiff, ever lives in his

successors, passes judgment and makes known the truths of faith to those who seek them, *therefore are the Divine declarations to be received in that sense in which they have been and are held by this Roman See of blessed Peter*, that mother and teacher of all Churches, which has ever preserved whole and entire the teaching delivered by Christ, *and which has taught it to the faithful, showing to all men the paths of salvation and the doctrine of everlasting truth.*

6. The first Provincial Council of Westminster, held in 1852, states: 'When our Blessed Lord exhorts us, saying, "Look to the rock whence you are hewn; look to Abraham your father," it is fitting that we who have received our faith, our priesthood, and the true religion, directly from the Apostolic See, should more than others be attached to it by the bonds of love and fidelity. *Therefore do we maintain that foundation of truth and orthodoxy which Jesus Christ willed should be maintained unshaken; namely, the See of Peter, the teacher and mother of the whole world, the Holy Roman Church. Whatever is once defined by it, for that very reason alone we consider to be fixed and certain;* and when we look at its traditions, rites, pious customs, discipline, and all its Apostolic Constitutions, we follow and cherish them with all the affection of our hearts. In fine, we of set purpose publicly declare our obedience and respect for the Pope as Christ's Vicar, and we remain united to him in the closest bonds of Catholic unity.'

7. Nearly five hundred of the bishops assembled in Rome to celebrate the Centenary of the Martyrdom of SS. Peter and Paul, in the year 1867, had no hesitation in addressing Pius the Ninth in the following terms: 'Believing that Peter has spoken by the mouth of Pius, whatever has been said, confirmed, and decreed by you to preserve the deposit of faith, we also repeat, confirm, and profess, and with one mind and heart we reject all that you have judged it necessary to reprove and condemn as contrary to divine faith, to the salvation of souls, and to the good of society. For what the fathers of Florence defined in their Decree of Union is firmly and deeply impressed in our minds—that the Roman Pontiff is the Vicar of Christ,

the head of the whole Church, the father and teacher of all Christians.'

The bishops of Italy and the Order of S. Francis sent in petitions of their own to the same effect.

14. On the 9th of February the Pontifical Commission of Postulates was summoned to decide whether this petition should be laid before the Pope. With hardly any dissent the decision was affirmative; and on the 7th of March an additional chapter was distributed to the Council, entitled: 'Chapter to be added to the Decree on the Primacy of the Roman Pontiff: That the Roman Pontiff, in defining matters of faith and morals, cannot err.'

Eighteen days were given to the bishops to study this *schema*, and to send in their amendments in writing before it would be proposed for discussion.

15. And here we will for a time leave the subject of the infallibility, and go back to examine the first Constitution on Catholic Faith, which, as we have seen, was unanimously passed by six hundred and sixty-seven fathers of the Council in the third Public Session. Thus far we have followed the historical narrative of events. We must now shortly examine the subject-matter of the first Constitution or Decree.

The following statement is a brief paraphrase of the first Constitution on Catholic Faith :—

It begins in its preface or introduction by enumerating

the evils which, since the Council of Trent, have sprung up in the world, and by infection have threatened also the peace of the Church. The first cause of all these evils the Council affirms to be the rejection of the divine, and therefore infallible, authority of the Church. The inevitable consequence of this rejection was to leave all matters of religion to be decided by the judgment of individuals; from this again has followed the multiplication of sects conflicting with each other, whereby the faith of many in Christianity has been wrecked. The Holy Scriptures were asserted three hundred years ago to be the sole fountain of Christian faith; but the Holy Scriptures are now rejected by many as myths. From this abandonment of divine authority and of revealed truth two main principles of error come: the one, Rationalism, which makes the human reason to be the test, the measure, or the source of all truth to itself; the other, Naturalism, which denies altogether the existence of a supernatural order of grace and truth. The legitimate offspring of Rationalism and of Naturalism are Pantheism, Atheism, and Materialism. These, in the order of the human mind, destroy even natural theism—that is, the belief of the existence of God and of the soul—and in the order of politics have brought in the lawless spirit of revolution, which is now undermining the foundations of human society. Such is the description given in the *schema* of the intellectual aberrations of the world outside the Church. But it goes on to say that many Catholics also, by contact with these errors, have lost, if not faith, at least piety and the Catholic instinct which is the legitimate antagonist of indifferentism. From which cause erroneous interpretations of the doctrines of the Church have been introduced, and the orders of nature and of grace, of human science and of divine faith, have been mixed and confounded together. The Constitution then proceeds to treat in four chapters—(1) of God, the Creator of all things; (2) of revelation; (3) of faith; (4) of the relation of faith and reason.

16. It may be asked why, in the nineteenth century of the Christian world, need an Œcumenical Council be convened to define these things? The answer is: Because these things are divine and vital truths, and because they have been denied. For three centuries these foundations of all truth have been undermined by systematic negations, which have now issued in a formal and widespread rejection of all faith. They who ask the question can have little knowledge of the intellectual history or the intellectual state of the so-called Christian world. They are not likely indeed to have much knowledge of the acts of Pius the Ninth, who, through the whole of his pontificate, has been striving to rectify the intellectual aberrations of these

later days. Every age has hitherto had its heresy. It may be said that the nineteenth century has no heresy, or rather that it has all heresies, because it is the century of unbelief. The intellect of man for three hundred years has broken loose from faith, and the heresy of the day is a heresy against the order of even natural truth; it is the assertion that reason is sufficient to itself. We, as compared with the men of the sixteenth century, have a great advantage. We see the whole intellectual movement which then began fully worked out to its legitimate conclusion. They saw only the first deviation from the path, which then was hardly appreciable. The reason of man either is, or is not, sufficient to itself. If it be, then Rationalism is its perfection. If it be not sufficient to itself, then somewhat higher than reason is needed. Or, in other words, reason is either its own teacher, or it needs a teacher higher than itself. The Christian world till the sixteenth century believed that the teacher of the reason of man is God, that the teaching of God is perpetual by the world and in the world, and that the reason of man is thereby related to Him as a disciple to a guide. The movement of the sixteenth century in its last analysis is the assertion that the reason of man is the critic and the measure of all truth to itself. The Reformation in all its diversities of national and personal character—German, Swiss, French, English,

Scottish—is all one in its principle. It consisted in an appeal from the living authority of the Church to the inspired Scriptures, or to the Scriptures with the written records of Christianity, tested and interpreted by reason. All particular controversies against particular Catholic doctrines or practices were no more than accessories and accidents to the main debate. The essence of the Reformation consisted in the rejection of the doctrinal authority of the Church. The Reformers denied it to be divine, and therefore unerring and certain. The history of the Reformed religion in Germany abundantly proves the truth of this assertion. It has had three periods. The first was a period of dogmatic rigour. The Lutheran doctrine was imposed and believed as the word of God. Men believed the Lutheran religion as they had before believed the Catholic, less only the principle. They had believed the Catholic doctrine to be the word of God; they now believed the Lutheran to be the word of God. They had believed the voice of the Church before; they believed the voice of the Bible now. It belonged to no individual to say what is the voice of the Church. But it was left for each to say what is the voice of the Bible. This period could not last long. Its own incompleteness suggested doubts. The contentions and contradictions of the Reformers shook the authority of the Reformation. Men of consecutive minds then began to give up dogma, and to withdraw into a personal piety. The second period was one of pietism, with a diminishing definiteness of Christian doctrines. But pietism, unsustained by the positive objects of faith, could have no duration in itself. It is like the seed which, having no root, withers away. It soon passed into the third period, which was one of Rationalism. Pietism hid its eyes from doctrines which it was tempted to doubt; but Rationalism looked them steadily in the face, and searched beyond them into the reasons, evidences, and authorities on which they rested. The search was soon over. It terminated in a book, and the book rested upon human history. Book after book of the Holy Scriptures was tried by Rationalistic criticism, and rejected until the whole Bible was banished to the realm of myths, and the Lutheran Reformation was ruined at its base. The Rationalists of to-day in Germany are the legitimate sons of the Lutherans of three hundred years ago.

17. What has happened in religion has happened also in philosophy. Three hundred years ago the intellectual system of the world was represented by the philosophy of the Christian schools. Philosophy was the intellectual prelude or avenue to the scholastic theology, and beyond all doubt this philosophy is the most solid and subtil system which the human in-

tellect has ever elaborated by its own unaided force. The Reformation revolted against both the scholastic theology and the scholastic philosophy. Precisely the same development of doubt, ending in scepticism, pantheism, atheism, and naturalism, has been the result. The line of philosophy from Leibnitz, Wolff, Kant, to Schleiermacher, Hegel, Fichte, Schelling, and Strauss, exhibits the same steady advance to the rejection of all that is above the level of reason or of nature. And yet the later German philosophy regarded itself as a theology. But it taught that reason cannot prove the existence of God—that the argument from design will yield to us, not God, but only a being great enough to make the universe. It teaches also that God is the world, and the world God; that all things are manifestations or emanations of God, and that God by a necessity creates or manifests Himself for His own justification; that He cannot reveal Himself to men by outward revelation or through the senses; that all materials of reason are derived only through the external world; that religious belief and religious feeling are one and the same; that faith is founded in the feeling of the reality of the ideal; that nothing is to be believed, nor can be required of man to believe, which is not capable of demonstration. These propositions were textually before the minds of those who elaborated the first Constitution on Catholic

Faith, for these and the like aberrations in philosophy had been spreading for generations through the German people. It is true that they were the offspring of Lutheranism, and existed formally in the non-Catholic schools; but it is to be remembered that in the mixed universities the Catholic and Protestant populations were confounded together, and that the government appointed Protestant professors, at whose lectures Catholics attended. Infection cannot be circumscribed, nor diseases kept within a ring-fence. The same habits of mind are found to pervade men of the same nation, and among Catholic philosophers unsound theories had begun to appear. Pius the Ninth, during his pontificate, has been compelled to condemn three or four philosophies which were being taught by Catholic professors.

18. With this short paraphrase of the Introduction, we will go on to the chapters of the Constitution *de Fide Catholica*, endeavouring to reduce to the narrowest compass the matter contained in it.

The Vatican Council in this Constitution has defined truths which have never been treated by any Council before.

In the first chapter it affirms that the creation of all things came from the free will of God, in exclusion and condemnation of the philosophies of emanation, manifestation, and pantheistic identity of God and the world, philosophic aberrations not yet extinct.

In the second chapter it affirms that the existence of God can certainly be known by the works of the visible creation. He has given us evidence enough, and reason to collect that evidence. This certainty of our natural reason may be called the infallibility of the natural order. God has so manifested Himself in creation that the reason in a normal state may come to know His existence, His power and divinity. This infallible certainty is the foundation of the moral life of man. St. Paul says that they who know not God by the things which are made are inexcusable. But they would not be inexcusable if God could not be known by the light of reason. And if in this knowledge the reason could be deceived—that is, if it were not certain — then there could be no moral obligation upon the conscience to believe. The atheist, pantheist, and sceptic, would all be excused for their doubt and unbelief. But if the existence and moral character of God be doubtful, the basis of all morals is doubtful too. *Lex dubia non obligat.* No Council of the Church has hitherto ever been compelled to make such a definition as this, for no age of the Christian world has yet so far departed from the theism which, from the beginning of the world under all perversions and corruptions, has pervaded mankind. It may be that in England surprise may be felt at such a decree; but nobody who knows Germany and France and the philosophies of this century will fail to understand the reasons of it, and to see its absolute need. It is here to be noted that the Council does not affirm that men must come, or ordinarily do come, to the knowledge, of God by the process of their own reason. It is certain, as a fact, that they receive this knowledge, from their earliest consciousness, by the instructions of others and by the doctrine of faith. The decree affirms two things—the one that the works of creation afford a sufficient evidence of the existence of God; the other that the reason has an intrinsic power of discernment by which that evidence may be collected into a logical proof. In this assertion two errors are excluded—the one which denies that the visible world presents an adequate evidence of the existence of God; the other that denies to the reason a power to read that evidence without the tradition and proposition of the truth. The second chapter, after vindicating these truths of the natural order, goes on to affirm the possibility and the fact of revelation; it affirms also that revelation is necessary to two things—first, that man may attain to the knowledge of truths above and beyond the order of nature, and, secondly, that by such revelation man may be raised to a higher order of knowledge and perfection.

It thereby denies that man can attain to such elevation and perfection of and by his own natural powers.

The third chapter opens with these words: "Forasmuch as man depends altogether on God, his Maker and Lord, and the created reason is wholly subject to the uncreated truth, we are bound to render to God in his revelation the full obedience of the intellect and of the will by faith." By this, again, the first axioms of Rationalism are denied. They cannot be better stated than in the words of the second and third propositions condemned in the Syllabus: "All action of God upon man and upon the world is to be denied." This would exclude revelation, grace, providence, and the dependence of the reason of man upon God by faith.

Again: "The reason of man, without any regard to God, is the sole judge of truth and falsehood, of good and evil; it is a law to itself, and is sufficient by its own natural powers to provide for the welfare of man and of nations."

The axioms of Rationalism may be thus stated: 1. Reason is the sole judge of truth, so that whatsoever it critically rejects is incredible. 2. Reason is the measure of truth, so that whatsoever exceeds its comprehension is incredible. 3. Reason is the sole fountain of truth, so that whatsoever is not found within its consciousness, nor can be elicited from it, is incredible. But if these axioms, or any one of them, be true, the reason of man is not dependent on God, and God cannot lay upon man the obligation of believing—that is, of faith.

From this it would follow that all revelation is needless, and that there is no truth except within the order of nature. But this denies all revelation, and therefore all supernatural truths such as the redemption, the Redeemer, the supernatural order of grace. There is no alternative but between Rationalism and faith. The human reason is either a critic or a disciple, and to determine this issue the first necessary truth to be proved is the existence of God. If the world be God, or if God be the world, or if the world be all, or if there be no personal Creator distinct from it, or if we cannot know Him to exist, then the reason of man is the critic of all that remains. All nature is under his feet, and though he cannot create a grain of sand or a corn of wheat he bears himself as if he were the lord and judge of all. Such is the ethical character of complete or absolute Rationalism.

But there is another form of Rationalism which is inconsistent and transitional. Many who would shrink from affirming that reason is the sole fountain of truth to itself, and that nothing is true which cannot be found in the human consciousness or elicited from it, nevertheless maintain that reason is the measure of truth, and that nothing which is incomprehensible is credible. The teachers of this school tell us that although without revelation many truths would not have been known to man, yet when once revealed they may be adequately comprehended and proved by reason, so that they become objects not only of faith, but of science. They therefore undertook to demonstrate the doctrines of the Holy Trinity and of the incarnation, which, when they had been reduced to the measure of reason, ceased to be the doctrines of revelation. This, especially in the last century, was the first momentum which carried many into unbelief of revelation altogether.

But if the truths of faith are not at the same time truths of science—that is, adequately measured by the reason and resolved into their first and self-evident principles—then there is an essential distinction between faith and science. Both are operations of the reason, and both are strictly rational, but they are distinguished by their subject-matter, and are therefore distinct in their principles. Faith is the obedience of the created intellect in dependence upon the uncreated intelligence of God. But faith is not a blind or irrational act. The motives and preludes of faith are processes of reason. Reason weighs the evidences which show that it is reasonable and rational to believe what the uncreated intelligence of God reveals to man. Faith comprehends, therefore, the reasons why it is a rational act to believe what it is beyond reason to discover. Science is the certain knowledge of truth in its principles. But this is possible to man only in the natural order.

In the fourth chapter the Council treats of the relation of faith and reason. It defines that there are two orders of knowledge, distinguished by their principle and their object—by their principle because the one proceeds by natural reason, the other by divine faith; by their object because the one is in the order of nature, the other in the order of supernatural truths. It then declares that between faith and reason there can be no conflict. They move on different planes, and truth can never be opposed to truth, nor can truth contradict itself; wherefore, if at any time there shall seem to be opposition between the doctrines of faith and the conclusions of reason, the conflict can only be apparent and transient, and while it seems to exist we are bound even by reason, which assures us of the certainty of faith, to believe the conflict to be not real, but only apparent.

The Constitution then further declares that faith and reason are mutually helpful:—

> Wherefore so far is the Church from opposing the cultivation of human arts and sciences that in many ways it helps and pro-

motes it. It neither ignores nor despises the benefits which flow from science into the life of men : it rather affirms that inasmuch as sciences proceed from God who is "the God of Sciences," so, if rightly handled, by the help of his grace they lead to God again. Nor does the Church forbid that such sciences should use their own principles and their own method within their own sphere ; but, while recognising this just liberty, it carefully guards the divine doctrines, lest they, in resisting error, receive it into themselves, or, by going beyond their own limits, the sciences should enter upon and disturb the things which are of faith.

It further says that the doctrine of faith is not a philosophical discovery, but a divine deposit to be faithfully guarded and infallibly declared by the Church.

If the Vatican Council had met and parted without any act beyond this one decree, it would have applied a direct and searching remedy to the intellectual aberrations of the nineteenth century. The proof of this may be seen in the outcry of unbelief against the Council. If it had not touched the quick, the outcry would not have been heard.

CHAPTER IV.

THE FIRST CONSTITUTION ON THE CHURCH.

THE additional chapter on the Infallibility of the Head of the Church was distributed, as we have seen, on the 7th of March, and in the last days of April the amendments of the bishops on the *schema* on the Primacy and the Infallibility of the Roman Pontiff were printed and distributed to the Council. The *schema* consisted of an introduction and four chapters, of which the first related to the institution of the primacy in the person of S. Peter, the second to its perpetuity in his successors, the third to the nature and character of the primacy, and the fourth to the infallibility attached to the primacy.

The general discussion on the *schema* opened on the 13th of May by a report of the Commission on Faith. It lasted through fourteen sessions—that is, from the 14th of May to the 3d of June. By that time it had become evident that the general discussion of the subject was exhausted. Not a new argument was to be heard; the old were endlessly repeated. The general discussion had anticipated even the special discussions on the chapters. Sixty-four had spoken. A hundred more had put down their names to speak. But inasmuch as there were five special discussions yet to come, in every one of which every one of the seven hundred members of the Council might speak—that is to say, in all, each one five times—it was obvious that to continue the general discussion was only to talk against time. The hundred bishops whose names were down had still the privilege of speaking each one of them five times more—that is, on the introduction and the four chapters. The remaining six hundred in the Council, besides, might do the same. In all human affairs the limits of common sense must be respected at last. By the regulations of the Council, or, as we should say, by the order of the House, any ten bishops might petition the presidents, not indeed to close the discussion, but to do, what any two members of our Legislature may effect, to put it to the vote of the whole Council whether the discussion should be continued or closed. A petition was sent in signed not by ten but by a hundred or a hundred and fifty bishops; and the question of closing was put to the Council, which, by an immense majority, closed the general debate.

Then began the special discussions. On the introduction and the first two chapters there was little to be said. On the introduction seven spoke, on the first chapter, five, on the second only three. On the 9th of

June began the debate on the third chapter, in which thirty-two spoke. The introduction, together with the first, second, and third chapters, and the amendments proposed, were then sent back to the Commission of Faith. On the 15th of June began the discussion of the fourth chapter—that is, on the infallibility, which occupied eleven sessions, during which fifty-seven spoke. No one asking permission to speak further, the discussion closed, and the chapter, with the amendments, was sent to the Commission as before. The whole time given to this discussion extended over nearly seven weeks—that is, from the 14th of May to the 4th of July. The introduction and the first two chapters were then reported and accepted almost unanimously. On the third chapter the amendments were seventy-two, which were reported on the 5th of July. Many were accepted, but many were further amended twice or three times, and the whole chapter was sent back once more to the Commission for further revision. Then on the 11th of July the report was made on the fourth chapter, relating to the infallibility, on which ninety-six amendments had been proposed. A new title and three new paragraphs had been added to it by way of introduction. On the 13th of July the third and fourth chapters were passed by a great majority. The whole *schema* was then printed again and distributed to the Council, and the final vote was taken. There were present 601 fathers of the Council. The *Placets*, or *ayes*, were 451; the *Non placets*, or *noes*, were 88; the *Placets juxta modum*, that is *aye* with modifications, were 62. These written amendments, to the number of 163, were sent as usual to the Commission. They were examined and reported on the 16th of July. Many were adopted, together with two amendments proposed by the commission. The whole was then reprinted and distributed, put once more to the vote, and passed.

In the same General Congregation a protest was read by the Cardinal President, which was to the following effect:—

MOST REVEREND FATHERS,

From the time that the Holy Vatican Synod opened by the help of God, the bitterest warfare instantly broke out against it; and in order to diminish its venerable authority with the faithful, and, if it could be, to destroy it altogether, many writers vied with each other in attacking it by contumelious detraction and by the foulest calumnies; and that, not only among the heterodox and open enemies of the cross of Christ, but also among those who give themselves out as sons of the Catholic Church, and, what is most to be deplored, even among its sacred ministers.

The infamous falsehoods which have been heaped together in this matter in public newspapers of every tongue, and in pamphlets without the authors' names, published in all places and stealthily distributed, all men well know, so that we have no need to recount them one by one. But among anonymous pamphlets of this kind there are two especially, written in French, and entitled *Ce qui se passe au Concile*, and *La dernière heure du Concile*, which, for the arts of calumny and the licence of detraction, bear away the palm from all others. For in these not only are the dignity and full liberty of the Council assailed with the basest falsehoods, and the rights of the Holy See denied, but even the august person of our Holy Father is attacked with the gravest insults. Wherefore we, being mindful of our office, lest our silence, if longer maintained, should be perversely interpreted by men of evil will, are compelled to lift up our voice, and before you all, most reverend fathers, to protest and to declare all such things as have been uttered in the aforesaid newspapers and pamphlets to be altogether false and calumnious, whether in contempt of our Holy Father and of the Apostolic See, or to the dishonour of this Holy Synod, and on the score of its asserted want of legitimate liberty.

From the Hall of the Council, the 16th day of July 1870.

   PHILIP, CARDINAL DE ANGELIS, *President*.
   ANTONINUS, CARDINAL DE LUCA.
   ANDREW, CARDINAL BIZZARI.
   ALOYSIUS, CARDINAL BILIO.
   HANNIBAL, CARDINAL CAPALTI.

Whether history will ever record by whose hands the works here censured by name were written cannot now be said. I am glad that it does not fall to my lot to reveal them. The Council had been enveloped for eight months in a cloud of all manner of publications, from pamphlets to articles in newspapers sufficiently near to the truth to impose upon the world at large, and so far from the truth as to be calumniously false. Nobody was spared. The chief torrent of misrepresentation broke upon the august head of the Church, and fell upon all that were near to him in the measure of their nearness. Not only acts which were never done, words that were never spoken, motives that were never thought of, were imputed to those of the majority whose duty forced them to choose truth before popularity. The majority in the Council was a minority compared with their assailants from without, who by every form of opposition attacked them through eight long months. But they were supported by two things—the consciousness that the unbroken tradition of Divine Revelation was at their back, and that the sympathy of the Catholic Church throughout the world surrounded them on every side. Therefore they were silent till the conflict was over, and the work was done. With this protest closed the 85th General Congregation of the Council. There remained only one further act, the fourth Public Session.

The summer heat had long begun to affect the health of the Council. Many of the bishops had been compelled by illness to return home; many were still in Rome, but unable to attend the sessions; some were dead. It was therefore desired by a great majority that the fourth Public Session should be held without delay. To this was added the daily expectation of war between France and Prussia. On the evening of the 17th, fifty-five bishops signed a declaration announcing their intention not to appear at the Public Session. On the next day it was believed that they left Rome. Tuesday, the 18th of

July, was fixed for the Public Session. It was held with all the usual solemnities, Pius the Ninth presiding in person. After the solemn mass the Holy Scriptures were placed open upon the lectern on the high altar, the *Veni Creator* was sung as usual. The Bishop of Fabriano then read the Decree *de Romano Pontifice* from the *ambo*, and the under-secretary of the Council called on every father of the Council by name to vote. Each, as his name was called, took off his mitre, rose from his seat, and voted. There were present 535; of these 533 voted '*Placet*, 2 only voted *Non placet*. The scrutators and the secretary of the Council, having counted up the votes, went up to the throne, and declared that all the fathers present, two only excepted, had voted for the decree. The Pontiff then confirmed the decree in the usual words. In a brief address to the Council he prayed that the few who had been of another mind in a time of agitation might in a season of calm be reunited to the great majority of their brethren, and contend with them for the truth. The words of the allocution were as follows :—

> Great is the authority residing in the Supreme Pontiff, but his authority does not destroy, but build up; it does not oppress, but sustain, and very often it has to defend the rights of our brethren the bishops. If some have not been of this mind with us, let them know that they have judged in agitation, but let them bear in mind that the Lord is not in the storm

(3 Kings xix. 11). Let them remember that a few years ago they held the opposite opinion, and abounded in the same belief with us, and in that of this most august assembly, for then they judged in "the gentle air." Can two opposite consciences stand together in the same judgment? Far from it. Therefore we pray God that He who alone can work great things may Himself illuminate their minds and hearts, that all may come to the bosom of their father, the unworthy Vicar of Jesus Christ on earth, who loves them, and desires to be one with them, and united in the bond of charity to fight with them in the battles of the Lord; so that not only our enemies may not deride us, but rather be afraid, and at length lay down the arms of their warfare in the presence of Truth, and that all may say with S. Augustine, "Thou hast called me into thy wonderful light, and behold I see."

The *Te Deum* was then sung, and the pontifical benediction closed both the fourth Public Session of the Council of the Vatican and a conflict which for centuries had troubled the peace of the Church. In the first voting on this *Schema* before the Public Session, 601 fathers of the Council voted. Of these 451 voted for the decree, 88 against it, and 62 for it *juxta modum*, or *aye* conditionally. In the fourth Public Session 535 voted: 55 absented themselves, which would raise the number to 590. Eleven were absent, from what cause is unknown; but as permission had been given some days before to leave Rome, they may have set out on their journey homeward. In the majority of 533 were included 52 of the 62 who voted *juxta modum*, or conditionally, in the last general congregation. This raised the 451 of that day to 503.

Therefore 30 who had been absent from the congregation had returned to vote in the last Public Session. The two bishops who voted on that day against the decree, as soon as Pius the Ninth had confirmed it, at once submitted and made a profession of their faith. They proved by their adverse vote the liberty which the 55 who left Rome equally possessed; and by their prompt submission they showed to the world that their opposition had been offered not to the truth of the doctrine, but to the expediency of defining it.

An English journal which throughout the Council laboured week by week to deride or to depreciate the Council and all its acts, described this closing scene in these words: 'The ceremony (of the 18th of July), taken as a ceremony, appears to have fallen very flat.' The Council had been for eight months engaged in something more than ceremonies. Such, however, was not the estimate of another witness.

> The *Placets* of the fathers struggled through the storm, while the thunder pealed above and the lightning flashed in at every window, and down through the dome and every smaller cupola. "Placet!" shouted his eminence or his grace, and a loud clap of thunder followed in response, and then the lightning darted about the Baldacchino and every part of the church and Conciliar Hall, as if announcing the response. So it continued for nearly one hour and a half, during which time the roll was being called, and *a more effective scene I never witnessed*. Had all the decorators and all the getters-up of ceremonies in Rome been employed, nothing approaching

to the solemn grandeur of the storm could have been prepared, and never will those who saw it and felt it forget the promulgation of the first dogma of the Church.*

Other critics saw in this thunderstorm an articulate voice of divine indignation against the definition. They forgot Sinai and the Ten Commandments.

Having closed the narrative of what passed in the Council, we must now turn back to notice what had been passing outside, and we must go someway into the past. We have already seen with what activity the Bavarian Government had endeavoured, from the spring of 1869, to bring down the united opposition of all the governments of Europe upon the Holy See before the Council assembled, and even to prevent its meeting. The Council was no sooner opened than the same policy was pursued by diplomatists in Rome. They were in intimate and constant communication with those who were in opposition within the Council. Many of them obtained every *schema* as it was distributed to the bishops. It is to be remembered that this fact proves the violation of the secret imposed on all who were within the Council, and in those who had sworn to its observance it involved perjury. One exception is to be made. An ambassador of a great Catholic power rejected every offer to obtain

* Times correspondent quoted in the *Vatican*, August 5, 1870.

K

for him the *schemata*, and when at last he desired to have some particular document, he wrote openly to the Secretary of the Council to ask for it. The document was at once sent to him with the assurance that whatsoever he desired should be at once placed in his hands. The *schemata* surreptitiously obtained were without delay published in the *Augsburg Gazette*. One of the least scrupulous of these agents expressed himself in these words :—

> The governments are by degrees acting an almost ridiculous part towards the Council. First boasts, then embarrassment, connected with meaningless threats ; and at last the confession that the right time has passed by, and that the *Curia* has command of the situation. If German science had not saved its position, and been able to establish a firm opposition in the Council, even in contradiction to its own will, and kept it alive, and if our Lord God had not also set stupidity and ignorance on the side of the *Curia* and of the majority, the governments would have been put to shame in the sight of the whole world. Prince Hohenlohe, in fact, is the only statesman possessed of a deeper insight in this question, and by degrees he has come to be looked upon as belonging to the minority.*

This inflated vain-glory neither needs comment nor is worth censuring. But it proves to all what ought to be known, how the bishops of 'the minority' were pursued and harassed by men of a lower mind, some being of the priesthood, and others of the laity who gathered in Rome to conspire and intrigue against the Council. They were well known, and

---

* Friederich's 'Diary,' p. 202.

their words and acts were noted; but inasmuch as they were not feared, they were let alone. A despatch was sent to Cardinal Antonelli on the 20th of February by Count Daru, then Minister of Foreign Affairs in Paris, for the purpose of preventing the definition. It was answered on the 19th of March in a reply which demonstrates that the notion of incompatibility between the infallibility of the Pope and the civil allegiance of subjects is a chimera. Ever since a Christian world existed, States have been in peaceful relations with an infallible Church. They have not cared to enquire whether the infallibility resided in the head, or in the body, or in both.

During the eight months of the Council, Rome was full of rumours as to the intentions of governments. It was believed that the French army would be withdrawn, and that the Italian Revolution would be let in. Letters came from France threatening the withdrawal of the French troops. When these tidings reached Pius the Ninth, he said to an English bishop, 'Do they think that the Vicar of Christ, unworthy as he is, can be moved by such threats?' Renewed attempts were made to induce the governments to join in a final and united pressure upon the Council, the effect of which was, as might have been foreseen, to demonstrate more clearly than ever that the supreme authority of the Church as the witness and teacher of Christianity was at stake. The necessity of the definition was once more forced by these facts upon those who for a while hesitated. After this there were in the Council only those who believed the definition to be inopportune, and those who saw it to be necessary.

It has seemed better to reserve until the end of this narrative a subject of which the adversaries of the Catholic Church have endeavoured to avail themselves in their warfare against it—that is, the attitude of a certain number of the bishops towards the decrees and action of the Council. Pomponio Leto, who writes as their friend and partisan, has done them a grievous wrong. His history reads like the history of a Parliamentary opposition. Such the world believed them to be, and tried to make them; but they were Catholic bishops, and the world was disappointed. The Council of the Vatican was held under obstructive and menacing circumstances of a kind to which no council was ever hitherto exposed. The world has opposed all councils, the civil powers have been often either openly or secretly hostile, but down to the Council of Trent, and the Council of Trent also included, no council has been the passive and silent butt against which the tongues and the pens of the world were so unceasingly levelled. The press of

Europe in all languages, and almost every day for eight months, discharged every weapon of ridicule, sarcasm, and misrepresentation against the Pope and the Council. Solid argument there was little indeed. But the world is more swayed by ridicule than by argument. The havoc made in France in the last century by the spirit of mockery is recorded in history as a terrible example of the deadly evil which can be wrought by so contemptible an agency. But there was in activity another and a darker power. The indiction of the Council had hardly been published when "Janus" appeared, true to his name, double-faced and double-tongued—a book more full of false accusations than any that ever came from nominally Catholic hands. Published in all languages, and greedily devoured by those who are not of the Catholic unity, no book has perhaps placed more stumbling-blocks in the way of men who were seeking the truth. The odium, suspicion, and prejudice excited by it in the minds of our separated brethren will cost many who were on the threshold of truth the grace which is beyond all price. In the face of these boisterous winds, the Council of the Vatican, trusting to its Divine Master, launched out into the deep. For eight months it held on its way without changing its course, bearing unmoved the stress of the storm. But though the Council was unmoved, individual men were shaken. We have seen before how governments and diplomatists were already in motion conspiring against the Council. "Janus" had told the world what the Council would do, and the civil powers were invoked by the same hands and voices to prevent its acts, or even to hinder its meeting.

When, therefore, at the outset of the Council, it was heard that a certain number of bishops had formed themselves into an opposition, the world and the newspapers, the non-Catholics outside the unity of the Church, and a small number of discontented or pretentious minds within it, thought that the Council was divided, and that Rome would be defeated. From that moment the press teemed with eulogies of the bishops who were supposed to be in opposition. They were learned, eloquent, far-sighted, noble-minded, manly, independent. The majority was a herd of ignoble, uncultured, servile, ignorant flatterers. The bishops of the opposition were mortified, day after day, by praise for words and acts they had neither done nor spoken; they were dishonoured by commendations for conduct which, as Catholic bishops, they abhorred. It was hardly possible for them to clear themselves without violation of the secrecy of the Council. They had to bear what members of Privy Councils and of Cabinets have to suffer—the eulogies which dishonour them at the expense of their colleagues

The True Story of the Vatican Council. 151

and the perversion of their conduct, which they cannot clear without a breach of integrity. Nevertheless, at last the bishops of Mayence and of Rottenburg were compelled to expose the falsehoods of their admirers.* Thus much it is necesssary to say

* "Mgr. Hefele and Mgr. von Ketteler have found it necessary to publish a statement with reference to documents which have appeared in the *Augsburg Gazette*. 'We can neither speak,' says the Bishop of Rottenburg, 'of what the *schemata* contain, nor of anything which is said by the orators in the general congregations. But it is evident that there are people, not bishops, but having relations with the Council, who are not restrained by duty or conscience. . . . The memorial of a certain number of German and Austrian bishops against the definition of infallibility ought not to have been published before it was presented to the Holy Father. I myself, who signed it, could not obtain a copy of it. Yet what has happened? Before the address was sent to the Vatican it was printed in the newspapers—I need not say to our great displeasure—and to this day we do not know how it was done. . . . . It is probable that the *auri sacra fames* has something to do with it.' The Bishop of Mayence also protests against 'the systematic dishonesty of the correspondent of the *Augsburg Gazette*.' 'It is a pure invention,' he observes, 'that the bishops named in that journal declared that Döllinger represented, as to the substance of the question, the opinion of a majority of the German bishops. And this,' the German prelate adds, 'is not an isolated error, but part of a system, which consists in the daily attempt to publish false news, with the object of deceiving the German public, according to a plan concerted beforehand. . . . . It will be necessary one day to expose in all their nakedness and abject mendacity the articles of the *Augsburg Gazette*. They will present a formidable and lasting testimony to the extent of the injustice of which party men, who affect the semblance of superior education, have been guilty against the Church.'"—From the *Vatican* of March 4, 1870.

"There was a time when I was a grateful disciple of the Provost Döllinger, and when I respected him sincerely. During several years I attended all his lectures at Munich. I was then of one mind with him on almost all the great questions of ecclesiastical history. At a later period, in 1848, we were associated together as deputies in the in order to protect a number of Catholic bishops from the claim laid upon them by the world as its servants, and to protest once for all that the motives,

German Parliament of Frankfort. Even at that date, when all the great questions of our time were so frequently agitated, I think that I coincided with him in his political views. I recognise with grief that there is now a complete opposition between the opinions of the Provost Döllinger and my own as to the substance of the question which actually occupies our attention. The Provost Döllinger has been publicly pointed out as having co-operated with the author of that libel which appeared under the name of 'Janus,' and which is directed against the Church; and we have no evidence that he has hitherto thought fit to declare, as an obedient son of the Catholic Church, that he does not share the opinions which animate that work. The book of 'Janus' is not only directed against the infallibility of the Pope, but even against his primacy, against that great and divine institution in the Church to which we owe so manifestly, by means of her unity, the victories of the Church over all her adversaries in all ages. 'Janus' is moreover a tissue of numberless falsifications of the facts of history, to which perhaps nothing but the 'Provincial Letters' of Pascal can be compared for violation of truth. And not only has the Provost Döllinger failed up to the present time to disavow his co-operation with the author of 'Janus,' but he is himself notoriously the anonymous author of the writing entitled 'Considerations presented to the Bishops of the Council on the Question of the Infallibility of the Pope'—a writing which is indeed much more moderate than 'Janus,' but which is nevertheless so perfectly similar to it in general tone of thought, and betrays aims so exactly identical, that the world has justly inferred a most intimate connection between the authors of 'Janus' and of the 'Considerations.' . . As to what concerns myself, and the notion that I may be one of those who agree with Dr Döllinger as to the substance of the questions most earnestly debated at this moment, I formally declare that nothing can be less true. I am in agreement only with the Döllinger whose lessons formerly filled his disciples with love and enthusiasm for the Church and the Apostolic See; I have *nothing in common* with the Döllinger whom the enemies of the Church and of the Apostolic See now load with praises.—† WILLIAM EMMANUEL, BARON VON KETTELER, Bishop of Mayence. Rom: February 8, 1870.'—From the *Vatican* of February 25, 1870.

conduct, and intentions of the bishops who opposed the definition of the infallibility, are to be judged not by the representations of newspapers, of non-Catholics, or of false brethren, but by their own words and actions.

As for the motives of those who opposed the act of defining, we have already seen that the arguments for and against the opportuneness of defining the infallibility were many and grave. No man would be a safe or competent judge of the arguments in favour of defining who could not also fully weigh the gravity of the arguments against it. These reasons have been amply given already in the last chapter, and they need not be repeated here. As for the motives which governed the fifty-five bishops who absented themselves from the fourth Public Session, we are bound to believe their word. Who should know their motives if they themselves did not? It is mere trifling, or worse, for others to pretend to know better. They tell us that they thought it unseasonable, inexpedient, and inopportune to make a definition. Posterity will believe them rather than their detractors, who are already forgotten or rejected as false witnesses. So much for their motives, which no man may judge, but God only; and when we remember who they were, and what some of them have done and suffered for conscience' sake, history will jealously protect them from the breath of the world, whether in slander or in praise.

But next as to their conduct. When Pius the Ninth first announced his thought of holding an Œcumenical Council, he not only invited but laid upon his counsellors, whether in Rome or from other nations, the obligation to declare to him as before God whether it was opportune to hold a Council, and what it would be opportune for the Council to treat. Everybody was then either opportunist or non-opportunist, for the main question was "what is opportune?" The Council was not called together to register edicts; it was convened for the purpose of discussion. Discussion, among mortals, means divergence of minds, and two sides at least. When the *schemata* were laid before the Council, Pius the Ninth expressly told the bishops that they were not his work, and did not bear the stamp of his authority. They were put into the hands of the Council to examine, discuss, amend, reject, and even "bury," as one said, if found to need interment. The Council had a liberty of speech so great that a bishop of one of the freest countries of the world said: "Our Congress has not greater liberty of discussion than the Vatican Council." Why then should it be turned to the reproach of any bishop if he used the right which the whole Council possessed? The bishops opposed freely whatsoever they thought to deserve it. The first Constitution on Faith was opposed, totally recast in form, but in doctrine was immutably the same; and it was finally passed by an unanimous vote of 667, including, therefore, the vote of every bishop who before had offered opposition. The *schema* of the Little Catechism was opposed. The "order" of the Council was opposed. It was amended and opposed again. The introduction of the infallibility into the Council was opposed. The *schema* was opposed at every stage in what may be called its second reading and in committee, and clause by clause. It was sent back, recast, and opposed again. In every stage of its progress those who dissented used their right and privilege, which may be called innate in a council or constitutional in a commonwealth, to oppose whatsoever they thought to be inexpedient or inopportune. In this certainly they were acting within the rights possessed by all members of the Council, and the exercise of this right was in itself legitimate.

But it may be said that they used their right too freely and with pertinacity when they saw, or might have seen, that an immense majority of the Council was opposed to them. It is not the duty of an historian to extenuate any fault, but he ought to be still more careful not to impute faults too readily. It is not to be denied that the Council—for by that term may rightly be described its great and united majority—judged that the privilege of opposition was used too freely in matters of an indifferent or unimportant kind, and that it was persevered in too long when it was evident that no legitimate result could be obtained. The Council saw, or believed itself to see, that after a certain date the inordinate prolongation of discussion could have no effect but to render the definition impossible, not by argument or reason, conviction or persuasion, but by the chapter of accidents or by talking against time. But this would be entering once more into the realm of intentions, which is under a higher jurisdiction than that of history. Looking back upon the Council after six years of strange and afflicting events, which have calmed and united the minds of those who were then opposed to each other, we are better able to weigh and appreciate the conduct of men as they acted either singly or together. Moreover, the memory of many among the foremost in those events gives a great solemnity to our judgment. The Archbishop of Paris was a man of great culture and intellectual gifts. The playfulness of manner with which he bore himself towards those who were most opposed to him took off all sharpness from the conflict in which they were mutually engaged. We then little thought of the vision of horror in which he was soon to be enveloped, and of the death which should so soon be inflicted on him *in odium Christi*. His heroic refusal for the sake of others to save his life has raised him to the fellowship of those who have won a martyr's crown. All this makes the task of history lighter. To this memory, again, must be added the noble fortitude of the German episcopate with the Archbishop of Cologne at its head. The bishops of Germany have won for themselves the dignity of confessors for the supreme and infallible authority of the See of Peter. They were the first to vindicate the Council of the Vatican by their courage. We might go further, and enumerate the great public services rendered by eloquence and energy to the Church in France by some who left the Council before the 18th of July. All these things weighed together will incline future historians to sum up the contest for the definition of the infallibility in some such way as this:—" Since the last Œcumenical Council a theological question of the gravest kind, relating to the doctrinal authority of the head of the Church, and therefore pervading his whole jurisdiction, had divided the minds of some in France, and partially also in Germany and in England. An Œcumenical Council was summoned to meet, in 1869, in Rome. Five hundred bishops in 1867 had affirmed in the amplest terms the doctrinal authority of the head of the Church. Of these the majority desired that in the coming Council all questions on this doctrine should be closed, and all future controversies ended. By word and by writing they declared their desire for such a definition. On the other hand, some who had joined in the acts of 1867, and had shared in the composition of the address, were of opinion that, as a matter of prudence, the subject ought not to be brought before the Council, or, if brought before it, should, as a matter of prudence, be set aside. For months before the Council assembled efforts were made on both sides, openly and without reserve, in public documents, in pastoral letters, in theological works, to promote or to prevent the definition. There was no concealment or intrigue on either side; it was needed by neither, it would have been worse than useless if it had been attempted. All was as open as a general election in England. On either side every act was known, and the desires and intentions of each side were manifest. Under such circumstances the Council met in December 1869. At once on both parts those who held for and those who held against this definition drew together. It was natural and legitimate that they should confer and unite, and form themselves into some kind of permanent combination. On which part this was done first no history can certainly tell, but the interval at most could only be that of a few days sooner or later. Those who were opposed to the definition were believed by the number of names attached to one of their petitions to amount to about 120. The first test of the number of those who desired the definition was by the month of February known certainly to be more than 450, for many declined to sign the petition who declared that if the definition were proposed they would give it a steadfast support. The two sides may henceforward be called the majority and the minority. Now, without doubt, on both sides there was often a feeling that some things ought not to have been said or done. Bishops are men, and men are liable to infirmities; nevertheless, the whole was conducted with perfect openness and in the light of day. It was a fair trial of reason, argument, and legitimate strength. The majority steadily grew greater, the minority steadily grew less. In the final and solemn vote, 533—that is, 33 more than the unanimous 500 of the Centenary— voted for the definition, 2 voted against it, and 55 stayed away, making in all 57 adverse votes. This was all that remained of the 120 supposed, but never known, to be in opposition. The majority was therefore all but ten to one." With these facts before their eyes men have no need to fetch about for intrigues and cabals to account for the action and result of the Vatican Council. It was a fair, open contest. About a tenth part of the Council endeavoured by argument, reason, influence, and the powers given to them by the order or procedure of the Council, to prevail upon the vast majority of their brethren, which was morally, indeed, the episcopate of the Church, to follow their guidance. The majority were unable to swerve from their conviction of what was not only most opportune, but of absolute necessity for the welfare of the Church, for the authority of its head, and for the certainty of its doctrine. The majority prevailed over the minority. The universal law of civilised life and of human society governed the Council of the Vatican. The minority were not wronged because the majority would not swerve. What injury was done to them if the Council declined to yield to the judgment or will of those who were only a tenth of its number? The only complaint that could be made would be that a majority would not yield to a minority; but would that complaint be just or reasonable?

Some adversaries of the Vatican Council have catered for the world with stories of violence, and outcries, and tumults. Among others an anonymous narrator, Pomponio Leto, who declares himself to be an outsider, and could therefore only speak by hearsay, is quoted as an eye-witness. He graphically describes the confusion of the cardinals, "who pulled their red hats over their eyes."* The cardinals had no hats, red or otherwise, and the eye-witness is convicted of fabrication. But it is not Pomponio Leto who says he saw this scene; it is the addition of those who have endeavoured to serve their hostility by destroying the honour of Cardinal Vitelleschi. In spite of repeated categorical denials from his brothers, Pomponio Leto is, for controversial purposes, still declared to be Cardinal Vitelleschi. Now the

* Controversialists and adversaries of the Catholic Church have asserted and reasserted with such tenacity, after reiterated contradiction, that the work entitled *Eight Months in Rome during the Vatican Council by Pomponio Leto*, was the work of the late Cardinal Vitelleschi, that it may be well to give an outline of the case.

On its publication in Italy some years ago it fell dead from the press; but when translated into English it fell upon a soil prepared by *Janus* and *Quirinus*. It was at once said that it was reported to be the work of Cardinal Vitelleschi; next, that it was probably so; then, that it was certainly so; finally, it was quoted without question or doubt as the work of the cardinal. None of this happened during his life; it began immediately after his death. Pope Honorius was declared to be a heretic forty years after his death--Cardinal Vitelleschi was declared to be Pomponio Leto as soon as he could not expose the imputation. The hope of setting one cardinal against another was a motive too strong to be resisted. The *Times* first began cautiously: the *Daily Telegraph* pushed on more boldly. The brothers of Cardinal Vitelleschi, hearing of this stain cast on the memory of their brother, wrote to expose its falsehood. Their words were published, but commented on as evasive; and the calumny was repeated. Next, on the 5th of July 1876, the *Guardian* reasserted and filled out the charge with circumstances. Then came the *Saturday Review*. Then the *Contemporary*, which over and over again says, "Cardinal Vitelleschi writes," "Cardinal Vitelleschi affirms," "Cardinal Vitelleschi tells us," &c. As if the two Marchesi Vitelleschi, brothers of the cardinal, had not pledged their honour in a public contradiction. Then the *Quarterly Review*, which, with a candour that stands alone, inserted in its first

L

cardinal certainly would not have talked about red hats. Nevertheless Pomponio Leto, who was inside when the cardinals pulled their hats over their eyes, was outside when the great tumult arose in which Cardinal Schwarzenberg was carried fainting from the *Ambo* to his seat. He saw, he tells us, the servants outside rushing to the doors of the Council, fearing for the lives of their masters. It is with such melodramatic and mendacious stuff that those who

number of this year a correction of this injurious error. But after all this, on the 24th of February 1877, the *Saturday Review*, as if nothing had happened, speaks of Cardinal Vitelleschi as regarding the decrees of 1870 with alarm and disgust. Cardinal Vitelleschi voted for those decrees on the 18th of July 1870. After all this it is not wonderful that the two brothers, Marchesi Vitelleschi, should write the the following letter with a just indignation :—

"Rome : January 8, 1877.

"I am grieved beyond measure that there should be in England anyone who still persists in the will to believe that the author of the book entitled 'Pomponio Leto' was my lamented brother, Cardinal Vitelleschi. At the end of June last year, 1876, a protest was inserted in one English journal, signed by us his brothers, in refutation of this odious calumny. I pray, however, that, if thought fit, this renewed protest be inserted in some newspaper, by which I repel, on the part also of my brothers, this most false assertion. And I declare, with full certainty of my conscience, that Cardinal Salvatore Vitelleschi was not in any way the author of the said book; so that whosoever shall say the contrary falsifies shamelessly, and can only say it to outrage the Church of which my deceased brother was a member without reproach.

"(Signed)   ANGELO NOBILI VITELLESCHI."

As to the true authorship of Pomponio Leto various things are affirmed. It belongs to the anonymous school of *Janus* and *Quirinus*, and seems to be the work of more hands than one, and to betray both a German and an English contributor.

wish to think evil of the Vatican Council are fed and duped.

But history has other witnesses to depend upon. Members of the Council who were never absent from its public congregations except about five or six times in all the eighty-five sessions have declared that no such scenes as Pomponio Leto, following the Italian papers, has described, ever took place. On two occasions the ordinary calm and silence of the Council was broken. In its sessions no applause was ever permitted, no expressions of assent or dissent were allowed. The dead silence in which the members had to speak contrasted strangely with all other public assemblies. It was like nothing but preaching in a church. But on two occasions the speaker tried the self-control of his audience beyond its strength. Strong and loud expressions of dissent were made, and a very visible resentment, at matter not undeserving of it, was expressed. And yet nothing in the Council of the Vatican went beyond or even equalled events of the same kind in the Council of Trent. It is indeed true that one excess does not justify another; but the events prove that when men deliberate on matters of eternal import, they are more liable to be stirred by deep emotions than when they are occupied with the things of this world. When the prelates at Trent heard a speaker say that the Archbishop of Salzburg claimed to confirm the elections of bishops, we read that they stirred up a mighty noise, crying "Out with him! out with him!" Others repeated "Go out! go out!" and others "Let him be anathema!" Another turned to them, and answered, "Be you anathema."* There may have been noise in the Council of the Vatican, but it did not reach this climax. Reference might be made to a certain debate on the 23rd of March in this year, 1877, when the majesty of the Commons of England lost itself in clamour, chiefly because a majority declined to let a minority have its way.

The axiom, "Where there is smoke there is fire," is sure enough. And these tales and tragedies could hardly have been invented if somebody by his imprudence had not made a momentary disturbance, and if the disturbers had not made more noise than they ought in their sudden heat. But in truth the Italian papers and the *Augsburg Gazette* are the chief sources of these mendacious exaggerations. An Italian paper gave in full the speech of Bishop Strossmayer, who was the subject of one of these Homeric commotions. In that speech he was made to apostrophise by name, as present before him and as a chief offender, a bishop who was not there at all to be apostro-

* Theiner, *Acta genuina S. Œc. Conc. Tridentini*, tom. ii., p. 606.

phised. When the speech had gone the round of Europe in a polyglot version, Bishop Strossmayer in a Roman paper denounced it as a forgery, and his letter has been reprinted again and again in England. Nevertheless the speech is reprinted continually to this day at Glasgow and Belfast, and sown broadcast by post over these kingdoms, and probably wherever the English tongue is spoken.

These details are given not to show that the Vatican Council was never disturbed, or that the Council of Trent was outrageous, but to show that, as it ought to be, a spot upon the rochet of a bishop is more visible than upon the broadcloth of a layman; and so, if a bishop or a council of bishops are for a moment stirred beyond their self-command, if for once or for twice in eight months there is a clamour such as happens almost every week in our Legislature, the world will dilate the fault into an outrage, and will deceive itself by its own exaggerations. It can be said with the simplest truth that not an animosity, nor an alienation, nor a quarrel broke the charity of the fathers of the Council. They were opposed on a high sense of duty, and they withstood each other as men that are in earnest; if for a moment the contention was sharp among them, so it was with Paul and Barnabas; and if they parted asunder on the 18th of July, it was only for a moment, and they are now once more of one mind and of one heart in the world-wide unity of the infallible faith.

And here we may leave the story of the Council. What remains is to examine the cause of all this tumult round about the Council, and in the governments and newspapers and non-Catholic communities of the world; for within the Council and within the Church the movement of men's minds was deep but still, and soon subsided into tranquillity, like the agitation of pure waters which return to their former calm and leave no sediment.

CHAPTER V.

THE DEFINITION OF INFALLIBILITY.

HAVING thus far completed our brief Story of the Vatican Council, we have only to examine the Definition of the Infallibility of the Roman Pontiff.

1. We will therefore first take the text of the fourth chapter of the first Constitution on the Church of Christ, in which is contained the infallibility of the head of the Church; and next we will examine its meaning.

CONCERNING THE INFALLIBLE TEACHING OF THE ROMAN PONTIFF.

Moreover, that the supreme power of teaching is also included in the Apostolic Primacy, which the Roman Pontiff, as the successor of Peter, Prince of the Apostles, possesses over the whole Church, this Holy See has always held, the perpetual practice of the Church confirms, and Œcumenical Councils also have declared, especially those in which the East with the West met in the union of faith and charity. For the Fathers of the Fourth Council of Constantinople, following in the footsteps of their predecessors, gave forth this solemn profession: The first condition of salvation is to keep the rule of the true faith. And because the sentence of our Lord Jesus

Christ cannot be passed by, who said : Thou art Peter, and upon this Rock I will build my Church,* these things which have been said are approved by events, because in the Apostolic See the Catholic Religion has always been kept undefiled and her holy doctrine proclaimed. Desiring, therefore, not to be in the least degree separated from the faith and doctrine of that See, we hope that we may deserve to be in the one communion, which the Apostolic See preaches, in which is the entire and true solidity of the Christian religion.† And, with the approval of the second Council of Lyons, the Greeks professed that the Holy Roman Church enjoys supreme and full Primacy and pre-eminence over the whole Catholic Church, which it truly and humbly acknowledges that it has received with the plenitude of power from our Lord Himself in the Person of blessed Peter, Prince or Head of the Apostles, whose successor the Roman Pontiff is ; and as the Apostolic See is bound before all others to defend the truth of faith, so also if any questions regarding faith shall arise, they must be defined by its judgment.‡ Finally, the Council of Florence defined : § That the Roman Pontiff is the true Vicar of Christ, and the Head of the whole Church, and the Father and Teacher of all Christians ; and that to him in blessed Peter was delivered by our Lord Jesus Christ the full power of feeding, ruling, and governing the whole Church. ‖

To satisfy this pastoral duty our predecessors ever made unwearied efforts that the salutary doctrine of Christ might be propagated among all the nations of the earth, and with equal care watched that it might be preserved genuine and pure where

---

* S. Matthew xvi. 18.

† From the Formula of S. Hormisdas, subscribed by the Fathers of the Eighth General Council (Fourth of Constantinople), A.D. 869. Labbé's 'Councils,' vol v. pp. 583, 622.

‡ From the Acts of the Fourteenth General Council (Second of Lyons), A.D. 1274. Labbé, vol. xiv. p. 512.

§ From the Acts of the Seventeenth General Council of Florence, A.D. 1438. Labbé, vol. xviii. p. 526.

‖ John xxi. 15-17.

it had been received. Therefore the Bishops of the whole world, now singly, now assembled in Synod, following the long-established custom of Churches,* and the form of the ancient rule,† sent word to this Apostolic See of those dangers especially which sprang up in matters of faith, that there the losses of faith might be most effectually repaired where the faith cannot fail.‡ And the Roman Pontiffs, according to the exigencies of times and circumstances, sometimes assembling Œcumenical Councils, or asking for the mind of the Church scattered throughout the world, sometimes by particular Synods, sometimes using other helps which Divine Providence supplied, defined as to be held those things which with the help of God they had recognised as conformable with the Sacred Scriptures and Apostolic Traditions. For the Holy Spirit was not promised to the successors of Peter that by His revelation they might make known new doctrine, but that by His assistance they might inviolably keep and faithfully expound the revelation or deposit of faith delivered through the Apostles. And indeed all the venerable Fathers have embraced and the holy orthodox Doctors have venerated and followed their Apostolic doctrine; knowing most fully that this See of holy Peter remains ever free from all blemish of error according to the Divine promise of the Lord our Saviour made to the Prince of His disciples: I have prayed for thee that thy faith fail not, and, when thou art converted, confirm thy brethren. §

This gift, then, of truth and never-failing faith was conferred by heaven upon Peter and his successors in this Chair, that they might perform their high office for the salvation of all;

---

* From a letter of S. Cyril of Alexandria to Pope S. Celestine I., A.D. 422, vol. vi. part ii. p. 36, Paris edition of 1638.

† From a Rescript of S. Innocent I. to the Council of Milevis, A.D. 402. Labbé, vol. iii. p. 47.

‡ From a letter of S. Bernard to Pope Innocent II., A.D. 1130. Epist. 191, vol. iv. p. 433, Paris edition of 1742.

§ S. Luke xxii. 32. See also the Acts of the Sixth General Council, A.D. 680. Labbé, vol. vii. p. 659.

that the whole flock of Christ, kept away by them from the poisonous food of error, might be nourished with the pasture of heavenly doctrine; that the occasion of schism being removed the whole Church might be kept one, and, resting on its foundation, might stand firm against the gates of hell.

But since in this very age, in which the salutary efficacy of the Apostolic office is most of all required, not a few are found who take away from its authority, we judge it altogether necessary solemnly to assert the prerogative which the only-begotten Son of God vouchsafed to join with the supreme pastoral office.

2. Such is the text of the decree about which before it came, and around which after it had been introduced into the Council, so vivid a conflict was waged. Let us quietly examine its meaning. We have seen that its title was changed from *De Romani Pontificis Infallibilitate* (On the Infallibility of the Roman Pontiff) to *De Romani Pontificis Infallibili Magisterio* (On the Infallible Teaching Office of the Roman Pontiff). The reason of this change was not only for greater accuracy, but because even the title of the decree excludes at once the figment of a *personal* infallibility. This, as it is imputed to the supporters of the definition, is a fable. The meaning of the title is explained in the first words of the decree. The *magisterium*, or teaching office, or doctrinal authority, is contained in the primacy. The supreme ruler is also supreme teacher. The primacy contains two things, the fulness of jurisdiction, and a special assist-

ance in the exercise of it. Now, under jurisdiction is contained the office of teaching. To deliver the law is to teach. The assistance of infallible guidance is attached to the *magisterium* or teaching office, and the *magisterium* is contained in the primacy. The infallibility is therefore attached to the primacy. It is not a quality inherent in the person, but an assistance inseparable from the office. It is therefore not personal, but official. It is personal only so far as the primacy is borne by a person. The primacy is not held in commission, as the office of Lord Treasurer or of Lord High Admiral. It is personal, therefore, only in the sense that the successor of S. Peter is a man and not a body of men—he is one and not many.

The Introduction then affirms that this doctrine has always been held by the Holy See, confirmed by the perpetual usage of the Church and of the Œcumenical Councils, especially in those by which the reunion of the East and West was for a moment effected.

In the fourth Council of Constantinople, which is the eighth of the Church, Pope Hadrian required the Eastern bishops to subscribe the creed of Pope Hormisdas, in which it is declared that the promise of indefectibility made to Peter is fulfilled in the fact that the Catholic religion has ever been preserved spotless in the Apostolic See.

In the second Council of Lyons the Greeks confessed that the Holy Roman Church had supreme and full primacy and principality over the whole Catholic Church, received from our Lord himself in Peter, prince and head of the Apostles, whose successor the Roman Pontiff is. The Profession of Faith then adds that the Roman Church " is bound above all Churches to defend the truth ; and if any questions arise about the faith, they ought to be defined (or finally determined) by its judgment."

The Council of Florence is still more explicit, as we have already seen ; but the words may be repeated in full because they are an implicit assertion of the doctrine of infallibility. The Vatican Council only defined explicitly what the Council of Florence had implicitly affirmed. From the acts of the Council of Trent it is evident that the infallibility of the Roman Pontiff would have been defined but for the state of the Council and the dangers of the times. The Florentine Council in 1439 says that "the Roman Pontiff is the true vicar of Christ and head of the whole Church, and is the father and teacher of all Christians ; and to him in blessed Peter the full power was given by our Lord of feeding, ruling, and governing the Universal Church."

The word "to feed" obviously means to feed with the Word of God, which is the food of the soul. But how shall he feed the Universal Church with this pasture of life if he cannot discern between what is food and what is poison—if instead of bread he be liable to give not only a stone, but the virus of falsehood? The Council of Florence, in using these terms, is reciting the words of our Lord to Peter, "Feed my sheep;" and in declaring the successor of Peter, as Vicar of our Lord, to be the teacher of all Christians, the Council did not so much as conceive the thought that he could mislead them from truth to falsehood, from life to death.

3. And here, in quoting the text of the Council of Florence, it may be well to anticipate the cavils of adversaries against the Vatican Council. It has been the practice of controversialists to charge Catholic theologians with truncating the decree, because in quoting it they commonly omit its last words, which run as follows: "Quemadmodum etiam in actis Conciliorum et sacris canonibus continetur" (*as is also contained* in the Acts of Councils and in the Sacred Canons). Anti-Catholic writers contend that the true reading of the decree is "quemadmodum et," *in that manner in which* it is contained in the Acts of Councils and in the Sacred Canons—intending thereby to prove, first, that the authority of the Roman Pontiff was created by Canons and Councils, and, secondly, that it is limited by them. To this it may be well to answer in two words.

First, supposing the true reading to be "*in that manner in which* it is contained," &c., this would not prove what they desire. The decree had already declared that the full power of feeding and governing was given to Peter, and in Peter to his successors, by our Lord himself. How then was it given by Canons or Councils? It was given before a Canon was made or a Council held. It is here declared to be of divine not of ecclesiastical institution, and it was given in full by our Lord in person. How can it be limited by Canons and Councils? It is itself the limit of Councils and of Canons, being limited only by its own Divine Author and by his continual assistance.

But next it is put beyond all doubt that the "quemadmodum et" is a corruption of "quemadmodum etiam," and that the meaning of the words is "as also is contained in the Sacred Œcumenical Councils and Canons;" that is to say, the statutes at large of the Catholic Church prove by record and testimony that the Roman Pontiff is vicar, and head, and pastor, and doctor of all Christians in the plenitude of power given to him in Peter by our Lord himself. It is a further corroboration of the doctrine declared in the decree. The whole history of the Councils and a series of Canons prove the fact. Now that this is the true reading is manifest from the following evidence. In the Vatican library there are three manuscripts of the Council of Florence. Every one reads not "et," but "etiam." One of them has a contraction of "etiam" which might easily be mistaken for "et;" but the others are written in full, and are clear beyond possibility of mistake. Again, in the Archive of the Vatican there is one of the originals of the Decree of Union. It has in parallel columns both the Latin and Greek text. It is signed by Eugenius IV. and by the Emperor Palæologus, and has the bulls or seals attached to it. In this "etiam" stands in full. Finally, at Florence is preserved the first of the four originals with the signatures of Eugenius and of the emperor, with the bulls of lead and of gold, and with the signatures of all the fathers of the Council of Florence. In this also the "etiam" stands in full, and the Greek text is identical in meaning. If then the clause is often omitted by Catholic writers, it is omitted as needless. After saying, "In the beginning God created the heavens and the earth," why should we add, "According as is contained in the history of the world?"

4. The decree then recites the action of the Pontiffs in all ages for the propagation of the faith among all nations, and for the preservation of its purity. It recounts the various ways in which this supreme oversight of the teacher of all Christians has been exercised. It declares that sometimes the bishops in

Synod, or singly one by one, following the immemorial custom of the Churches of the Catholic unity—for, as Tertullian says, "what is found in all places is not error, but tradition"—have faithfully guarded the form of primitive order, especially when any new peril threatened the dogma of faith, by bringing their causes or controversies to the Apostolic See. This they did "that the breaches of the faith might be repaired," as St. Bernard said, "by the authority in which faith cannot fail." These are the words of St. Bernard, but they ought not to be new to Englishmen, for they are almost the words of two Archbishops of Canterbury. St. Thomas, in a letter to the Bishop of Hereford, asks:—

> Who doubts that the Church of Rome is the head of all the Churches and the fountain of Catholic truth? Who is ignorant that the keys of the kingdom of heaven were entrusted to Peter? Does not the structure of the whole Church rise from the faith and doctrine of Peter?

St. Anselm almost anticipates the decree of the Council of Florence. He writes as follows:—

> Forasmuch as the providence of God has chosen your Holiness to commit to your custody the [guidance of the] life and faith of Christians and the government of the Church, to no other can reference be more rightly made, if so be anything contrary to the Catholic faith arise in the Church, in order that it may be corrected by his authority.

Sometimes the Pontiffs have proceeded by consultation with the bishops dispersed throughout the world, of which we have a recent example in the definition of the Immaculate Conception and in the preparation for the Council of the Vatican. In the former case, which related to a question of faith, every bishop throughout the world was required to send his judgment in writing on two points—first, whether the doctrine of the Immaculate Conception was definable, and, secondly, whether it ought to be defined. In the latter case, which was a question of opportuneness or of prudence, a certain number only were at first consulted. Sometimes again, the decree says, the Pontiffs have called all the pastors of the world to meet and to consult, as in Œcumenical Councils. Sometimes, it adds, the Pontiffs have proceeded to declare the faith by the Councils of particular Churches or provinces, as when St. Innocent the First, in the fifth century, confirmed the decrees of the Councils of Milevis and of Carthage on Original Sin. No other definition of this doctrine was made until the sixteenth century by the decrees of the Council of Trent. Again, St. Gelasius, in the year 494, by his supreme authority declared the number of the Canonical Books. The Canon of Holy Scripture rested on that pontifical act without any decree of an Œcumenical Council until the definition of the Council of Trent in the year 1546.

5. The Introduction further goes on to preclude by

anticipation many misconceptions of the doctrine of infallibility. It is hard to believe that some who have written on this subject really meant what they said. Some have called it the "apotheosis"* of the Pope. Possibly they did not know Greek. Some have said that he was deified—that is, made to be God. Probably they did not know what they said. Some have said that the decree made the Pontiff to be a Vice-God. If they meant *Dei* or *Christi vicarius*, many generations of Christians have said so before them, and we feel it no reproach; if they mean a substitute for God, or an idol, we may charitably doubt their sanity, or not unjustly suspect their truthfulness. Others again have said that to declare the Pontiff to be infallible is to invest him with divine attributes. The Jews said truly, "Who can forgive sins but God only?" And yet our Lord breathed upon his apostles and said,

* The use of the word *deification* in this controversy may be said to have come from a source which is not Christian. It first appeared in the correspondence from Berlin in one of our chief journals. The name of the correspondent was no secret; and he must have enjoyed the irony of using a Christian newspaper in England to assail the vicar of the Nazarene. From this beginning it was soon spread. One of the most recent and most flagrant instances is the following:—"The Vatican Council was so far the culminating yet utterly incomplete act, in a drama elaborately arranged, step by step, to finish with the deification of the occupant of the See of Rome." (*Times*, February 17, 1877.) It is to be feared that this writer did know Latin; and it would be well if editors knew the ridicule cast upon them on the Continent for these malevolent absurdities.

"Whosoever sins you forgive they shall be forgiven unto them." Did He invest them with divine attributes? If they say yes, then the infallibility, though it be a divine attribute, may be communicated. If they say no, they may be left to the care of friends, Anglican and Greek; or if indeed they believe with neither, why should they busy themselves about the Catholic faith? A man must be a Christian at least to be heard on the subject of the Catholic religion, or, to be just, he ought to believe at least in the infallibility of the Church before he contends about the infallibility of its head. Such controversy is like a Deist objecting to the inspiration of the Bible. But leaving all these extravagances, which belong properly to the region of newspaper correspondents, we will come to the difficulties of candid and Christian minds. Some have thought that by the privilege of infallibility was intended a quality inherent in the person whereby, as an inspired man, he could at any time and on any subject declare the truth. Infallibility is not a quality inherent in any person, but an assistance attached to an office, and its operation is not to give out answers as may be required by an interrogator, nor to know or to make known new truths, or to communicate new revelations. It is an assistance of the Holy Ghost whereby Peter's faith was kept from failing either in the act of believing or in the object of his belief, and through Peter the same assistance attaches to the office he bore, so that his successor in like manner shall be kept from departing from the traditions of faith committed to his custody. Its operation is therefore not the discovery of new truths, but the guardianship of old. It is simply an assistance of the Spirit of Truth, by whom Christianity was revealed, whereby the head of the Church is enabled to guard the original deposit of revelation, and faithfully declare it in all ages. All Christians profess to believe in the advent and presence of the Spirit of Truth, and in the promise that He shall abide with us for ever. Infallibility is the result of that presence. He preserves for ever His own revelation, not as a disembodied theory of disconnected doctrines, but as a whole in the visible witness and audible voice of the Church and of its head.

The Council of Trent has declared that the faith is the doctrine which our Lord delivered by word of mouth, and the Holy Ghost revealed to the apostles. Whatsoever, therefore, is not contained in this revelation cannot be matter of divine faith. It further declares that this revelation has been preserved by the continual succession of the Catholic Church.* The office of the Church, therefore, is to declare what was contained in that original revelation, and infallibility

* Sess. iv.

is the result of a divine assistance whereby what was divinely revealed in the beginning is divinely preserved to the end. Of two things one at least: either Christianity is divinely preserved, or it is not. If it be divinely preserved, we have a divine certainty of faith. If it be not divinely preserved, its custody and its certainty now are alike human, and we have no divine certainty that what we believe was divinely revealed. This is the issue to which men must come at last. The definition of the infallibility of the head of the Christian Church means this, and no more than this; that God, who revealed His truth, has founded His Church for the custody and perpetuity of His truth, and that He has made provision that His Church shall never fail in its custody, nor by error in its declaration cause the perpetuity of faith to fail. The visible Church is the highest witness among men for the original revelation of Christianity, both by its historical testimony and by its divine office. Reject this, and where is there divine certainty left on earth? But for the present we are engaged with the literal meaning of the decree.

6. The Introduction proceeds to describe infallibility to be "*a charisma of indefectible faith and truth.*" By this again the notion of a "personal" infallibility is excluded. The word *charisma* is used to express not a *gratia gratum faciens*, as theologians say—that

is, a grace which makes the *person acceptable* in God's sight—but a *gratia gratis data*, or a grace the benefit of which is for *others*, such as prophecy or healing, and the like. Now these gifts, as may be seen in Balaam, Caiaphas, and Judas, were not graces of sanctification, nor gifts that sanctified the possessor. They were exercised by men whose sin is recorded for our warning. By this also is excluded another misconception, if indeed any sincere mind ever entertained it—namely, that if Popes are infallible they are therefore impeccable; that if they cannot err in faith, they cannot sin in morals; that if their intelligence be guided by divine light, their will must be necessarily conformed to divine grace. But it is to be doubted whether any man in good faith was ever so confused in mind. To be impeccable is to be confirmed in the sanctifying grace which makes men acceptable before God. To be illuminated or guarded from error may co-exist with the sin of Caiaphas, who was a prophet, and crucified the Redeemer of the world. The decree says that this *charisma* was given by God to Peter and his successors that in the discharge of their office they might not err. It does not even say that it is an abiding assistance present always, but only never absent in the discharge of their supreme office. And it further declares the ends for which this assistance is given—the one that the whole flock of Christ on earth may never be misled, the other that the unity of the Church may always be preserved. Unity of faith generates unity of mind, unity of heart, unity of will. Truth goes before unity. Where truth is divided unity cannot be. Unity before truth is deception. Unity without truth is indifference or unbelief. Truth before unity is the law, and principle, and safeguard of unity. Unity of communion is the effect of unity of faith. The decree then assigns the reason of the definition. It says: "In these days, when the effectual authority of the apostolic office is especially needed, there are not a few who diminish it and speak against it. Therefore, because it is a divine truth, and because it has been contradicted and denied, we judge it to be altogether necessary to declare with all solemnity the prerogative which the Divine Founder of the Church has seen fit to *unite* with the *supreme pastoral office*." It seems hardly credible that men with these words before their eyes should impute to the Vatican Council the doctrine of personal infallibility, that is, of infallibility inhering in the person.

7. Thus far we have spoken of the introduction of the decree. We now come to the definition itself, which runs in these words:—

> Therefore, faithfully adhering to the tradition received from the beginning of the Christian faith, for the glory of God our

Saviour, the exaltation of the Catholic religion, and the salvation of Christian people, the sacred Council approving, we teach and define that it is a dogma divinely revealed: that the Roman Pontiff, when he speaks *ex cathedrâ*—that is, when in the discharge of the office of pastor and Teacher of all Christians, by virtue of his supreme Apostolic authority, he defines a doctrine regarding faith or morals to be held by the Universal Church—is, by the divine assistance promised to him in blessed Peter, possessed of that infallibility with which the Divine Redeemer willed that his Church should be endowed for defining doctrine regarding faith or morals; and that therefore such definitions of the Roman Pontiff are irreformable of themselves, and not from the consent of the Church.

The definition declares that the doctrine of the infallibility of the successor of Peter is a tradition from the beginning of the Christian faith; it then declares that doctrine to be contained in the divine revelation. Let it be noted that the definition rests itself not upon any inspiration, or consciousness, or conviction of any person, even of the head of the Church. It affirms a given doctrine to be a tradition from the beginning, and therefore to be revealed. But an objector may say, "How can that be known? who can tell what tradition is from the beginning?" Certainly no individual, nor any aggregate of individuals, can tell us this; they cannot exhaust the evidence of the Christian Church. But the Church itself can, and does, know its own evidence and its own tradition. It knows its own present and its own past with a living consciousness like that by which we know our own personal identity. No one outside us knows us as we know ourselves within. S. Paul asks, "What man knoweth the things of man but the spirit of man that is in him?" This is a simple fact of nature and of common sense. The attempt to dispute us out of a belief of our personal identity would consign our adversary to the Commissioners of Lunacy. How is it, then, that men can dispute with the Catholic Church as to its lineal traditions, which are recorded in its living consciousness? And yet it is not on this merely natural reason that the definition is founded; it rests upon the faith that the Divine Founder of the Church has promised to its head that he shall never err in declaring what is divine tradition, and therein what is divine revelation. And so S. Paul continues after the words already quoted, "What man knoweth the things of man save the spirit of man that is in him? Even so the things of the Spirit of God no man knoweth but the Spirit of God." It is by a divine promise and by a divine assistance that the Church never departs from the truth of revelation; and that promise was made to Peter not for his own sake alone, but for the sake of his brethren; and the promise made to Peter was made in him to all his successors in the headship of the Church, for the sake of the successors of the apostles and of the whole Church of which he is the chief pastor and teacher.

It is to be now further observed that the Council of the Vatican expressly quotes the decree of the Council of Florence, and as we have seen that the early Councils unfolded in succession that which was in germ before, making implicit truth explicit, so does this definition. It explains and defines what the Council of Florence meant by saying that the Roman Pontiff is "the pastor and teacher of all Christians." The definition says that he is so when he speaks *ex cathedrâ*, and he speaks *ex cathedrâ* when he defines anything of faith and morals to be held by the Universal Church. The phrase *ex cathedrâ*, though long used in theological schools, was for the first time here inserted in a decree of an Œcumenical Council. Its meaning is plain. "The Scribes and Pharisees sit in Moses' seat," *in cathedrâ Moysis;* they spoke in his place and with his authority. The *cathedra Petri* is the place and the authority of Peter, but the place and the authority mean the office. All other acts of the head of the Church outside of his office are personal, and to them the promise is not attached. All acts, therefore, of the Pontiff as a private person, or as a private theologian, or as a local bishop, or as sovereign of a State, and the like, are excluded. They are not acts of the primacy.*

* *The Centenary of S. Peter and the Œcumenical Council*, p. 59. (Longmans.) *Petri Privilegium* P. iii. 103.

The primacy is in exercise when the teaching of the Universal Church is the motive and the end, and then only when the matter of the teaching is of faith and morals. In such acts the promise made to Peter is fulfilled, and a divine assistance guides and guards the head of the Church from error. The definition declares that he then is possessed of the infallibility with which our Saviour willed to endow his Church.

8. Now it is to be here remembered that all Catholics believe the Church to be infallible in faith and morals —that is, that the Church is so divinely guarded that it never departs from the divine tradition of revealed truth. This all Catholics believe; no one who denies it is a Catholic. Whosoever doubts it ceases to be a Catholic. But this doctrine has never been defined. It needs no definition. No definition could make it more certain or more universal in its reception. Why then was the infallibility of the head of the Church defined? Simply because it had been denied by some; and, lest it should be denied by more, through the apparent impunity granted to the denial, the definition has put it beyond doubt. No one who denies it now is a Catholic; they who doubted it before were in an error which was at least proximate to heresy. They who doubt it now cannot be cleared of formal resistance to the divine authority of the Church. Such is the meaning of the words, "If any

contradict this our definition, which God forbid, let him be anathema."

9. In this definition it is explicitly defined that the head of the Church is infallible, and it is assumed as certain that the Church also is infallible.

It is declared that this infallibility extends to all matters of faith and morals, but it is not defined where the limits of faith and morals are to be fixed. It is defined that the acts of the head *ex cathedrâ* are infallible, but cases may perhaps arise in which doubts may be made as to whether this or that act be *ex cathedrâ* or no. In these cases of doubt no one can decide but the head of the Church. *Cujus est condere, ejus est interpretari.* The legislator alone is interpreter of the law. It was for this reason that Pius the Fourth, by a bull after the Council of Trent, first reserved to himself the interpretation of the decrees of the Council: secondly, prohibited all private persons to undertake to fix the meaning of them; and thirdly, excommunicated all persons who should appeal from the Council of Trent to a future General Council. If, therefore, any doubt be ever mooted as to whether an act be or be not an act *ex cathedrâ*, no one need be scared by those who, either to ventilate their learning or to alarm the simple, pretend that there are thirty theories as to what s or is not an act *ex cathedrâ*. The answer is simple. Ask no one but the author of the act. Half the controversies and nearly all the pretentious censures of the Vatican Council, if men would take this course, would die of inanition.

10. There are only two other points to be touched upon in this narrative. But they are too important to be passed over in silence.

The one is that in the end of the definition it is affirmed that the doctrinal declarations of the Pontiff are infallible in and *of themselves*, and not from the consent of the Church. That is to say, they are infallible by divine assistance, and not by the assent or.. acceptance of the Church to which they are addressed. Or, more simply, the teacher is not infallible because the taught believe his teaching. They believe his teaching to be true because they believe their teacher to be infallible. The motive for these words is obvious. They were the critical difference between what must be called once more by names which now have lost both meaning and reality, the Ultramontane and the Gallican doctrines. They are taken textually from the Four Articles of 1682.

A moment's reflection will justify the definition.

If the certainty of the teaching depends upon the assent of the taught, what becomes of the teacher?

If the consent of the Universal Church is to be obtained before a doctrine is certain, how is it to be done? Is it to be the consent of the bishops only, or of the priests also, or of theologians, or of the faithful, or of all together? And from what age? If the *ecclesia discens* is to confirm the *ecclesia docens*, no member of it ought to be disfranchised. Manhood suffrage is too narrow. Woman suffrage is not enough. All above the age of reason might fairly claim a vote. But as reading and writing have been proposed as qualifications for electoral suffrage, perhaps the Catechism might be required as a qualification. If the consent of the Church is to be obtained, it must be waited for. And how long? Who shall fix the days, weeks, months, or years, and what if there be no unanimity, mathematical or moral, after all? And how long is it to be waited for, and in the meanwhile in what state are the doctrines defined? Are they of faith or not of faith? is anybody bound to believe them, or nobody? are they the means of salvation or not? Can any surer way be taken to render all doctrine doubtful at least, if not odious to reasonable men? Open questions are bad enough, but suspended questions are worse.

The other point to be noted is the fact that this *schema* on the Roman Pontiff was originally the tenth and eleventh chapters of the *schema* on the Church of Christ. It was, as we have seen, taken out of the general *schema* on the Church, and, with the addition of the chapter on the infallibility, it was made into a *schema* by itself. But further it was decided that the *schema* on the Roman Pontiff should be brought on before the other. It may be asked, Why was this change of order made? In answer we may call to mind that in like manner the first *schema* on Catholic faith had been set aside, and out of eighteen chapters four only had been cast into a new *schema* by itself. It was found that the prolixity and vastness of the original *schema* gave no hope of its being discussed, unless everything else should be made to give way. Therefore such points as had never been hitherto defined, and such truths as at this time are both especially contradicted and vitally necessary to the very foundations of the faith, were selected for immediate treatment. We have already seen this in the last chapter. These topics, therefore, could not, without grave danger, be postponed. The rest might well be deferred. For instance, the fall of man, original sin, grace, the Incarnation, the Holy Trinity, have all been defined, but the religion of nature, revelation, faith, the relation of faith to reason, have never been defined; and they are the truths on which the Gnosticism, illuminism, and intellectual aberrations of the nineteenth century have especially fastened.

It was therefore most wisely decided to do first what was most wanted, and to do it speedily and surely.

11. The same is precisely true of the first *schema* on the Church of Christ. It was prolix and multifarious. It contained fifteen chapters. Much of its contents had been already implicitly or even explicitly defined. Its chief points, as, for instance, the infallibility of the Church, have never been denied or even doubted by any Catholic.

But as to the Roman Pontiff, the discussions on the third and fourth chapters, the number of the speakers, the multitude of amendments will show what was the mental anxiety even among the pastors of the Church. Certainly, then, it was wisely determined to define first the truths which had been denied, to declare that which had been contradicted, to settle that which had been in controversy, before treating of those things in which all men were agreed.

Besides, to treat of the whole *schema* of fifteen or (as it became) sixteen chapters, in the time still remaining to the Council, was impossible. It was foreseen that the summer heats would cut short the work of the Council before August. We have already

The True Story of the Vatican Council. 193

said that many were ill ; many more were only able by an effort to bear the strain of the Council. The rumours of impending war were continually becoming louder and nearer. It was therefore decided, at the petition of a large number of the bishops, which number might without trouble have been doubled, to bring into immediate discussion the subject by which for centuries the Church had been disquieted. We have seen how the minds of the bishops since the Centenary of St. Peter had been fixed upon it. From the outset of the Council it had been the motive of an open, legitimate, and honourable contention of two opposing sides. It was evident that the subject of the infallibility was always on the horizon. Every discussion was troubled by its shadow ; time was wasted ; discussions were prolonged beyond need or reason. A general secret uneasiness, such as is sometimes seen to prevail in legislatures where everybody is thinking of the same subject, which some hope for and others fear, and nobody dares to utter first, but of which everybody betrays a consciousness, kept the two sides in the Council in a state of mutual suspicion and needless antagonism. For the sake of truth and peace and charity, it was therefore determined to bring the subject into the light of day, and to sift and bolt it to the bran. If those who thought the defining of the infallibility to be inopportune could justify their judgment, then let it be adopted. If the contrary counsel should prevail, then it was to be hoped that it would be accepted. At all events, the only way to weigh, sift, and decide was to discuss openly and deliberately the contending reasons of this great debate.

But there was yet another motive of singular force urging the speedy commencement of this discussion. Seven hundred bishops of the Catholic Church assembled when the Council met; 667 had voted in the second Public Session; the number had been somewhat lessened by death and by departures; but more than half the Catholic episcopate was still in Rome. If the subject of the primacy and of the infallibility of the Roman Pontiff was ever to be discussed, it ought to be discussed in the fullest assembly of the episcopate. In no council before had so many bishops met together; in no future Council, it might be, would such a multitude ever meet again. Let the discussion then be taken not by surprise, not after the Council had been diminished in numbers, but when it was at its fullest strength. If the subject had been postponed till the numbers were reduced, adverse historians might have said that the bishops did not venture to bring on the debate while the Council was full; that they waited till it had dwindled to a manageable number who could be manipulated or overawed into a servile submission, and that then they defined the infallibility of the Pope. The higher and more manly course was chosen. It was resolved to bring on the trial of debate at once, and, as the event proved, the discussion was not begun a day too soon. It was only by a pressure which fell heavily upon every member of the Council, and with double weight upon the members of the Commission on Faith, who were compelled to meet after every congregation of the Council which multiplied its fresh amendments, that the Constitution on the Roman Pontiff was completed. It was confirmed and promulgated twenty-four hours before the breaking out of the Franco-German war.

12. Having now come to the end of this brief story of the Vatican Council, it may not be out of place to add a few words on the consequences which have either followed or have been supposed to follow from it.

Six years are now past since the 18th of July, 1870, and certain effects of the Council are already manifest, and many are imputed to it.

We will take first certain supposed consequences which the *Post hoc propter hoc* school affirm to be effects of the Vatican Council. For example, we have been told by a cloud of newspaper articles, and lately by a laborious German writer, that the Franco-

German war was caused by the Vatican Council. If we were not aware that the Goodwin Sands were caused by Tenterden Steeple, that assertion would be at least improbable, if not incredible. But no one who had watched the attitude of France and Prussia for many years had any need of the Vatican Council to explain the causes of that lamentable conflict. It is only a wonder that it did not happen before. To ascribe to Ultramontanes or to Jesuits the origin of that rivalry must be seen to be absurd by any one who reflects that the first effect of such a war must be the withdrawal of the French troops from the Roman State, and that the withdrawal of those troops was the instant cause of the seizure of Rome by the Italian armies. Jesuits and Ultramontanes are usually thought to be far-sighted in matters of this world; but if with their eyes open they did not foresee these consequences they would be unjustly credited with common sense. France and Germany went to war because the animosities of generations, the memories of wrongs endured and inflicted, the jealousy of rivals, and the covetous desire of territorial annexation common to both had stimulated the war spirit to an uncontrollable intensity. No Vatican Council was needed to drive them together, because no power on earth could have averted their murderous collision. But sometimes these events are paraded as the Nemesis on Papal pride.* The history of the Pontiffs, then, has been one long Nemesis, for none have ever suffered so often or so much; but their history runs up into a divine event in which the suffering for truth and justice became the law of the Church and of its head for ever.

13. It is not, however, to be denied that since the Vatican Council there has been an almost universal rising against the Catholic Church. It began with the Liberal party in Germany, and with the Liberals of Berne and Geneva, and with the Liberal party in Belgium, in Spain, in France, in Italy, in Brazil, and with some who call themselves Liberals in England. Catholics were told that they were denationalised, that they could be loyal only at the expense of their religion, that their allegiance was divided, and that they depended on a foreign head. All this was said by Liberals, and to the modern Liberal party are due the Falck laws and the fining, imprisoning, deposing, exiling of bishops in Germany and in Switzerland and

* "The same year which saw the overthrow of Cæsarism immediately after the plebiscite witnessed also the Nemesis which overtook the spiritual pride of the Pontiff, now exalted to its highest pinnacle, and showed to him who arrogated to himself *a divine nature*, that God is a jealous God, who will allow to none other the honour due to Himself."
—Geffken, *Church and State*, vol. ii. p. 334. Does this learned author know what a "divine nature" is? or does he believe that the Vatican Council declared Pius the Ninth to be *uncreated?*

in South America. To the Liberal Government of Italy is now due the Clerical Abuses Bill, or the Italian translation of the Falck laws. Herr Lasker is reported to have said that in Berlin he was the only Liberal left. The Vatican Council seems to have laid a Circean spell upon the Liberal party. They have put off their former nature, and have changed places with persecutors. The *Chiesa libera nello Stato libero* needs, as Liberals say, a supplement in the *Codice Penale*. Modern Liberalism is the Cæsarism of the State. Liberalism seems to believe that "all power in heaven and on earth" was given to it—that the State has power to define the limits of its own jurisdiction and also those of the Church. All sin and blasphemy against God is forgiven to men. There is only one unpardonable sin. Any one who speaks a word against the omnipotence of the State is disloyal, and shall never be forgiven. We were told in the Italian Chamber that *the law against the abuses of the clergy* was provoked by the Vatican Council. In the same breath the author of the bill and the members of the commission tell us that the same laws existed in the Penal Code of Sardinia before the Vatican Council was convened.

Quo teneam vultus mutantem Protea nodo?

M. Gambetta, the other day, made a funeral oration over the Gallican liberties. He told the Assembly that the National Church of France existed no longer —that the Vatican Council had denationalised it. These gentlemen, who receive the name of the Redeemer of the world with roars of laughter, are of such delicate theological perception as to be offended by the Vatican Council. If things are to be called by their Christian names, this is hypocrisy. There can indeed be little doubt that the Vatican Council has so drawn together the array of the Catholic Church as to make the anti-christian revolutions of the Continent feel the pressure of the great moral power which sustains the order of the world. Hence come not tears, but ravings.

14. Another supposed consequence of the Vatican Council was the "Old Catholic Schism." And here in justice it must be said that the opposition of governments and political parties was not spontaneous or without instigation. We have seen with what perseverance the fears of statesmen and cabinets were worked upon, and we know how ubiquitous and how subtil has been the activity of the international Revolution. But another cause was open and palpable. The "Old Catholic" schism in Germany appealed to the civil power, and the civil power promptly recognized and copiously paid its ministers. It seemed to bring the promise of a German National Church, representing the mind of the nation and without de-

pendence, as Dr Friedbergh has it, on "the man outside of Germany." But the "Old Catholic" schism was not the consequence of the Vatican Council any more than was Arianism the consequence of the Council of Nicæa. The definitions of the Council were indeed the occasion of the separation of a small number of professors and others from the unity of the Church, whose antecedents had for years visibly prepared for this final separation. The strange medley which met at Augsburg and Bonn and Cologne, of Rationalists and Protestants, and Orientals and Jansenists and Anglicans, was not the consequence of the Vatican Council. Every sect there represented had been for generations or for centuries in separation and in antagonism to the Catholic Church. The Vatican Council may have awakened a sharper consciousness of the cause of their separation, and a handful of such Catholics as composed *Janus* and *Quirinus* invoked their help to give the appearance of numbers. Even Pomponio Leto had too much wit to be there.

Before and during and after the Council formidable prophecies of separations to come, sometimes in tones of compassion, sometimes in tones of menace, were heard. And those who were most firm in urging onward the definition of the infallibility were not unconscious of the danger. They remembered that after the Council of Nicæa eighty bishops separated from the unity of the faith, and carried multitudes with them. Nevertheless the fathers of the Nicene Council did not forsake or compromise the truth, nor think it inopportune to declare it. S. Athanasius was reproached for dividing the Christian world for an iota. But that iota has, under God, saved the faith of the ever-blessed Trinity. The faith of the Christian world rests at this day upon the definition of Nicæa.

So again, after the Council of Ephesus, thirty bishops followed the Nestorian heresy. The fathers of that Council foresaw the danger, but they knew that no danger was to be compared with the danger of betraying the truth. They defined the doctrine of faith as to the unity of the One Person in two natures, and on that definition the doctrine of the incarnation has rested immutably to this day.

After the Council of Chalcedon the Monophysites separated themselves from Catholic unity.

Will any reasonable man say that the Arian, Nestorian, and Monophysite heresies were the consequence of the Councils of Nicæa, Ephesus, and Chalcedon?

But lastly, at the Council of Trent, the motives of human prudence and the pleadings of natural charity must have been very powerful on the side of endeavouring to win and to conciliate. Whole nations were on the brink of separation. But an Œcumenical

Council is not like a human legislature. It cannot suppress, or soften, or vary, or withhold the truth on calculations of expediency, or with a view to consequences. Necessity is laid upon it. As it has received, so it must declare. Deviation from the truth would be apostacy; silence when truth is denied is betrayal. This is what, it seems, Honorius did, and what some would have had Pius the Ninth do. Truth is not ours, it is of God. We have no jurisdiction against it or over it. Our sole office to truth is to guard it and to declare it. "That which ye have heard in the ear, preach ye on the house tops." For this cause the Council of Trent defined every doctrine which had been unhappily denied or distorted in controversy from the year 1517. It ranged its decrees along the whole line of the Lutheran aberration. Was the Lutheran separation the consequence of the Council of Trent?

15. After the close of the Council of Trent, the separations which were foreseen became complete. Whole kingdoms fell from the unity of the faith. But from that hour the Council of Trent has renewed and governed the Catholic Church. It may be said with truth that as the Council of Nicæa has guarded the faith of the Holy Trinity to this hour, so the Council of Trent has guarded both the doctrines assailed in the sixteenth century, and the discipline

of the Church in its manifold contacts with the world. The Church has been reproached as Tridentine. No greater honour could be paid to the Council of Trent. The Church is Tridentine in the sense in which it is Nicene, and in which it will henceforward bear the stamp of the Vatican Council. Every Œcumenical Council leaves its impress upon it, and all these impressions are clear and harmonious. The Church is not like a *codex rescriptus* in which the later writings obliterate or confuse the former, but like the exquisite operations of art in which the manifold lines and colours and tints are laid on in succession, each filling up what the other begins, and combining all into one perfect whole. But it is certain that after the Councils of Nicæa and of Trent the Arian and the Lutheran separations made many to fear lest evil had been done, and to doubt the prudence of the Council. They who had been brought up before the new definitions probably died in the belief that they could have gone on safely without them. And they who measured all things only by their own needs thought them to be unnecessary, and gave at most a cold submission to what had been decreed; so it might be now. But we must not measure all events]by ourselves, nor must we make our own times so much the centre of all things as to think what is needless to us cannot be needed by others now and hereafter. Œcumenical Councils look not at individuals only, but at the whole Church, and not at what may be needed by any one so much as what the truth demands. Men who speak in this way forget, or do not believe, that the Church is a witness and teacher. They look, too, only at the moment. But when the generation of to-day is past, and they who may have opposed or reluctantly acquiesced in what was not familiar to their youth are passed away, when the definitions of the Vatican shall have pervaded the living world-wide faith of the Church like the definitions of Nicæa and of Trent, then it will be seen what was needed in the nineteenth century, and what the Vatican Council has accomplished. Then in due time it will be perceived that never was any council so numerous, nor was ever the dissentient voices relatively so few; that never was any council so truly œcumenical both in its representation and in its acceptance; that never were the separations after it fewer, feebler, or more transient; and that never did the Church come out from a great conflict more confirmed in its solidity, or more tranquil in its internal peace. Those who love to declaim that the Council of the Vatican has divided the Church will no doubt go to the grave with the same illusions on their brain and the same assertions in their mouth. But they will have no succession. Facts win at last. The prophecies of separations which were to follow have come to nought, and the prophets are silent in the presence of visible unity. The Church is "unresting, unhasting." It hears calmly the counsels of its adversaries and the compassion of those who wish it no good; but it holds its peace. Time works for it. If science can say, "Hominum commenta delet dies, naturæ judicia confirmat," the Church can say, "Cælum et terra transibunt, verba autem mea non præteribunt."*

When the passions of men are laid by the silent lapse of time which stills all conflicts, noble and ignoble, history will reject as a fable, and censure as an indignity, the suspicion that the Council of the Vatican was convoked by Pius the Ninth chiefly if not altogether to define the infallibility of the Pope, and that they who promoted that definition were impelled by any motive but fidelity to truth. But, whatsoever may be their lot, they will count it to be one of the greatest benedictions of their life that they were called to help in the least measure to vindicate the divine authority of the head of the Church from the petulant controversies which had in these last centuries clouded with the doubts of men the steadfast light of divine faith. The definition of the infallibility of the head of the Church has put beyond controversy that the Church speaks for ever by a

* St. Matt. xxiv. 35.

divine voice, not intermittently by General Councils, but always by the voice of its head. It has met the unbelief of the nineteenth century by the declaration that the prophecy of Isaias and the promise of God to the Divine Head of the Church are for ever fulfilled in his vicar upon earth. "My Spirit which is upon Thee, and my word which I have put in thy mouth, shall not depart out of thy mouth, nor out of the mouth of thy seed or of thy seed's seed from henceforth and for ever."*

* Isaias lix. 21.

www.ingramcontent.com/pod-product-compliance
Lightning Source LLC
Chambersburg PA
CBHW031816220426
43662CB00007B/668